What peopl

FLESH

"Want to reimagine what impact your actual life—not only your beliefs—could have on others? Let Hugh Halter's masterful storytelling and laser-focused challenges guide the rest of your life with God. Your soul, and those around you, will be transformed."

Mindy Caliguire, director of Soul Care
with Willow Creek Association

h is as raw and authentic as the stories you encounter in *Flesh*. compelling, not just for its prophetic call for the church, but als how it gives us a vision of what it is to be human and to follow in t footsteps of Jesus."

Alan Hirsch, author of *The Permanent Revolution*

"Hugh r does it again. *Flesh* is *the* go-to book for an incarnational life."

Brandon Hatmaker, author of *Barefoot Church*

"In *Flesh*, Hugh Halter shows us how to help people find their way back to God. This is the kind of book that will not only change you but will show you how to gracefully change the people around you!"

Dave Ferguson, lead pastor of Community
Christian Church a piritual
entrepreneur th NewThing Network

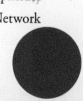

"*Flesh* is Hugh Halter's life. It's his best effort to date because this is him. And his life will challenge yours to be more like God in the flesh."

Carl Medearis, author of *Speaking of Jesus*

"By layering story upon story, Hugh creates a very compelling call for the church to take real people in real settings seriously. This story must be told so that the story of your life will come alive."

Deb Hirsch, coauthor of *Untamed*

"Hugh has a unique gift of making the familiar into the relevant and practical. *Flesh* blends both into a compelling, challenging must-read for every Christ follower."

Roger Cross, president emeritus of Youth for Christ/USA

"*Flesh* will reintroduce you to the reality of the incarnation. I love this book because it moves the 'missional' conversation from the classroom to the streets."

Dave Runyon, coauthor of *The Art of Neighboring*

"All I can say is that *Flesh* is a wonderful book—charming and warm-hearted, yet passionate and prophetic."

Michael Frost, author of
The Road to Missional and
The Shaping of Things to Come

"I loved this book! With characteristic humor, down-to-earth style, and an abundance of stories from his own life, Hugh opens our eyes to what Jesus has done for us in the incarnation and how it transforms us into being 'human like Jesus.' Hugh's passion to connect people to Jesus is contagious, and his relational and nonreligious way of doing so is refreshing."

Mike Breen, director of 3DM

"My friend Hugh has done it again! He cuts through the religious stuff to get to the point: living life here and now—on earth as it is in heaven. One of the greatest needs in the life of a post-Christendom church in North America is a richer understanding of the incarnation of Jesus and the implications His life has for daily living. In the book *Flesh*, Hugh provides both a fresh way of thinking about why Jesus took on flesh and gives us practical ideas that challenge how we live everyday lives in the kingdom."

Brad Brisco, author of *Missional Essentials* and *The Missional Quest*

FLESH

Bringing the Incarnation Down to Earth

FLESH

Learning to Be Human Like Jesus

HUGH HALTER

David C Cook®
transforming lives together

FLESH
Published by David C Cook
4050 Lee Vance View
Colorado Springs, CO 80918 U.S.A.

David C Cook Distribution Canada
55 Woodslee Avenue, Paris, Ontario, Canada N3L 3E5

David C Cook U.K., Kingsway Communications
Eastbourne, East Sussex BN23 6NT, England

The graphic circle C logo is a registered trademark of David C Cook.

Some names have been changed throughout to protect privacy.

The website addresses recommended throughout this book are offered as a
resource to you. These websites are not intended in any way to be or imply an
endorsement on the part of David C Cook, nor do we vouch for their content.

Unless otherwise noted, all Scripture quotations are taken from the Holy Bible,
New International Version®, NIV®. Copyright © 1973, 2011 by Biblica, Inc.™ Used
by permission of Zondervan. All rights reserved worldwide. www.zondervan.com.
Scripture quotations marked ESV are taken from The Holy Bible, English Standard
Version® (ESV®), copyright © 2001 by Crossway, a publishing ministry of Good
News Publishers. Used by permission. All rights reserved; NLT are taken from the
Holy Bible, New Living Translation, copyright © 1996, 2007 by Tyndale House
Foundation. Used by permission of Tyndale House Publishers, Inc., Carol Stream,
Illinois 60188. All rights reserved; NKJV are taken from the New King James Version®.
Copyright © 1982 by Thomas Nelson, Inc. Used by permission. All rights reserved.
The author has added italics to Scripture quotations for emphasis.

LCCN 2013953099
ISBN 978-0-7814-0997-1
eISBN 978-1-4347-0750-5

© 2014 Hugh Halter
The Author is represented by and this book is published in association with the
literary agency of WordServe Literary Group, Ltd., www.wordserveliterary.com.

The Team: John Blase, Nick Lee, Caitlyn Carlson, Karen Athen
Cover Design: Amy Konyndyk
Cover Photo: Veer Images

Printed in the United States of America
First Edition 2014

1 2 3 4 5 6 7 8 9 10

112613

TRAVEL GUIDE

Foreword by Jen Hatmaker   11
Introduction: A Tattoo into the World 13

INCARNATION **21**
    1. Nostalgic God   25
    2. Spiritual Vertigo   39
    3. A New Gospel   49
    4. Incarnational Lies   61

REPUTATION **75**
    5. Baby/Boy/Bloke   79
    6. Opening Act   97
    7. Workers' Comp   113
    8. Turning Tables   131
    9. Public House   145

CONVERSATION **161**
    10. When Grace and Truth Collide   163
    11. Speaking of Jesus   175

CONFRONTATION **187**
    12. The Wild Goose on the Loose   189

TRANSFORMATION **199**
    13. Finishing the Work   201

SKIN DEEP **211**

Notes 219

FOREWORD

I suppose when you boil all of life's wins and losses down to the real issues, you'll run into theology. I know that sounds weird, but it's true. Life is about God. Everything is about God. It can be said that *the* most important thing about each and every one of us is what we believe about God—and more specifically, what we are convinced about regarding Jesus. If He remains a historical figure who came to pay for our sins, then we may put a cross around our neck, we may go to church on occasion to thank Him for what He did for us, but we may not look much different from the guy or gal next door. But if you become convinced that Jesus had other reasons for coming to earth—namely to teach humans how to be human—then … well, you might just become a different human.

Flesh brings Jesus down to earth in ways that may help you finally understand who Jesus was—and even more importantly, what His life can be like in your life. As Hugh says in this book, Jesus didn't come just to die for your sins. He came to teach you how to live a full, earthy, gritty, and marvelous life.

Let's talk a bit about Hugh. He's my friend. My husband and Hugh are Harley buddies; my oldest son shot Hugh in the back with

11

a high-powered air rifle, dropping him to the ground; we've shared hundreds of glasses of wine together (not all at one time), spoken on the same stages together, and even cruised around Italy together with our spouses. And Hugh not only helps me and thousands of others understand the beauty of the life of Jesus but shows me Jesus in the way he lives.

Here's some stuff this book says that no other book does: You need to pick more fights in public. Stop trying to be godly, and instead try to be more human in the way of Jesus. Working a job or caring for your family is more spiritually important than doing a book study of Romans. And every home can be a pub. (Hugh has some big feelings about things, and you'll just have to read more to decode all of this.)

Hugh helps us read between the lines of theology and find the real man, the real God who lives next door—and as we do this, we'll discover a new way of living, a new way of being loved. This isn't a narrative on how to be more righteous or how to please God or how to get more things right. God never asked us to be right; He asked us to be real. I suspect Jesus is the good news most of us are starving for. It's just that He has been hijacked by rules and structures and humans afraid of grace.

If I could get a few books into the hands of every Christ follower—books that could change the entire paradigm of who a Christian is and what Christianity could be—*Flesh* would be in that short stack. This book could change everything, but perhaps more importantly, it can change you. May you discover the God of flesh who came to earth, saved our lives, and set us free forever.

Jen Hatmaker

INTRODUCTION

A Tattoo into the World

And the Word became flesh and dwelt among us. (John 1:14 ESV)

I never thought I would be here ... with her ... doing this.

It's 11:00 a.m., and I'm sitting in the lobby of Sean's Tattoo Parlor. It's a rather classy joint, but a tattoo joint nonetheless. No, it's not the way I usually spend family time, but today is different. I'm chaperoning my daughter McKenna as she gets inked for the first time. I don't want to get into the perplexities of parenting and permanent body art, but I felt compelled to support her decision. See, I've got a little color myself—a rendering of the earliest Celtic cross surrounded by the story of Isaiah 61 is etched on my right shoulder.

While Sean is working on McKenna, I voice my fear that she will want more tattoos and then ask, "So why do you think people tend to get so many tattoos, Sean? And why is the art of tattooing growing exponentially around the world?" Sean stops the vibrating needle, looks up at me, and says, "Because it's something permanent etched on someone's flesh that can't be stolen, taken away, or corrupted. It's unique to them, deeply irrevocably theirs, and represents a story that has formed them or at least means something to them. When someone lets me etch something meaningful into their dermis, that means a lot to me and should mean even more to them. Skin matters a lot."

Sean's words are more true than even he knows. What happens to our flesh stays on our flesh. If it's a scar, it stays. If it's our natural color, it stays. Our skin is us to others. It's what they see, and since our skin is able to bend and move, tighten and loosen, it is able to communicate hundreds of unique emotions, feelings, and thoughts. You can't hide your skin. Most of our nerve endings are in our skin, so what happens to our flesh is usually obvious to someone watching us. We feel the world through our skin, and our flesh is the front door to our emotions. Our flesh is the most vulnerable part of our bodies and oftentimes the reason we get judged, abused, enslaved, or stereotyped. Flesh matters!

Therefore, to have skin is to be human, and that's why *flesh* becomes the single most important theological, cosmological, and practical essence of our faith. Here's why.

God as Spirit intentionally put on skin for us.

This is called the *incarnation*—a word that means "to take on flesh."

DOCTRINE THAT MAKES SENSE

Just a few weeks ago, I was curious about this topic and dug through some old boxes of theology books and journals from my seminary days. I found a huge black notebook that held all my writings and thoughts regarding "doctrine"—the doctrine of predestination, the doctrine of election, the doctrine of end times, just to name a few. I was taught that these were the central issues of faith and therefore that I was required to know the concepts and supporting scriptures intimately. Back then I remember thinking, *Really ... these are the biggies? These doctrines that we fight about, leave churches over, judge one another for, and really can't figure out anyway?*

Today, after twenty-five years of pastoring and training leaders from over a hundred denominations that split off or started new denominations because they couldn't see eye to eye on some of these "critical" doctrines, I still feel the same way. Those doctrines are important ... but not central. They can help us know Jesus, but they can also hinder us from knowing Him. Jesus is what is to be central, and He is the person people are really looking for.

Here's the deal. People are not looking for doctrine. They're looking for a God with skin on, a God they can know, speak with, learn from, struggle with, be honest with, get straight answers from, and connect their lives to. Some of my closest friends are ex-churchgoers or nominal Catholics, Protestants, Buddhists, and Muslims, and I can tell you for certain that they aren't looking for greater clarity on theology unless that theology really tells them who God is, what He is like, what He thinks of them, who they are, and what their lives can become. People want to find God with skin in the game!

This is why I'm writing this book. People need to know what the incarnation of God is. This one "doctrine" must become central because it not only tells you exactly what God is like but also shows you how big a life you get to live. As you understand the incarnation of Jesus, all the false notions about what Christianity is will become clear. You may even find that the incarnated Jesus isn't a big fan of any organized religion and that your life lived in His life doesn't have to have any relics of religion at all. The incarnation will teach you how to parent your children, how to love your spouse, what to focus your life's efforts on, and how to follow God without all the crap. The incarnation is what those inside and outside the Christian faith are looking for, and if every Jesus follower truly "got it," it would fix every negative stereotype people have about Christians, Christianity, and the church. The incarnation of Jesus will give you proof that God understands how hard it is to be human, and it will help you see how to be human to the fullest. This new *fleshy* faith will help you be the least judgmental person your friends will meet and will guide you into the street-level kingdom life you've always wanted to live. It's a big deal!

This is a picture of a tattoo that is now on my left forearm. I saw the image while walking down a street in West Bank Palestinian Bethlehem. You know, the city that we sing about at Christmas, where we picture serene, silent nights and nativity scenes of peaceful animals, mangers, and wise men. Now Bethlehem has a huge cement wall around it, symbolizing what's worst in human-religious relationships brought about by religion. As I personally saw the pain of separation, I was deeply inspired by this illustration that shows God wanting to come down from the heavens and enter or reenter the city He created. That ladder represents the incarnation, and I hope that as you keep reading you will allow the ladder of Jesus's life to reenter your world. As John 1:51 says, "The Son of Man … is the stairway between heaven and earth" (NLT).

This thought from Dallas Willard changed how I began to see everything: "Jesus teaches you to live your life as He would live your life."[1] What an amazing possibility! As we walk through these pages, you will find that is exactly the opportunity you have. Galatians 2:20 says, "I have been crucified with Christ; it is no longer I who live, but Christ lives in me; and the life which I now live in the *flesh* I live by faith in the Son of God, who loved me and gave Himself for me" (NKJV). Once you understand the incarnation of Jesus, I believe you will find some remarkable possibilities. First, He is able to live your life, and second, you are in turn able to live His—not completely in either direction but full enough and close enough that your imagination will come alive to a much larger vision for why you exist on this planet.

HOW TO READ THIS BOOK

I wrote this book in the order that God came to us. If being a disciple of Jesus means that we know what He knows and we learn to live like He lived, it makes sense to follow His cadence. The grid below will be a guide. It shows the flow, timing, order, and process of how Jesus moved into the lives of people. In short, incarnation leads to a good reputation, which leads to a conversation, which leads to natural confrontation and then transformation.

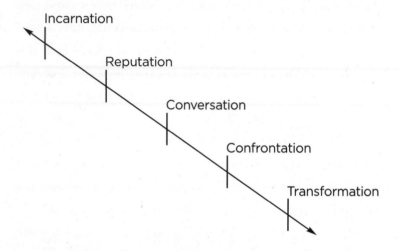

Each of these five sections will begin with a short description to let you know where we're going. At the end of each chapter, I'll provide questions I would use if I wanted to challenge myself or a group of friends who are processing with me. In fact, I think you will get a lot more from the experience if you invite some friends to join you as you work your way through this.

Think. Did you ever learn about the main New Testament doctrine of the incarnation as you grew up in church? If not, what did you grow up thinking was the main thing?

Feel. Do you ever feel like you got short sheeted in organized religion or churchianity? What type of emotions do you feel when you think of a God who became human so that you would understand Him?

Do. Consider approaching this book like a brand-new story. Go buy a new Bible so that you can follow along in a fresh way. Also, email a few friends and see if they want to go through this with you.

INCARNATION

It'd been a long day, and I could hardly lift my head off the smoke-stained headrest in the taxi. My flight to Chicago got in late, and to make my first engagement I hastily jumped out at what I thought was the right address. The cab pulled away, and after a few minutes I realized I was off by one number; the right number was two miles away. Bummer. I couldn't find another cab, so I decided to drag my suitcase down the busy streets near Wrigley Field for about thirty minutes.

On my way, a few folks asked me for food, money, or liquor. One woman asked if I needed any "love." As soon as I said, "No, thank you," I looked up and almost became entangled between two gay men who were locked deeply in a public display of affection. I sashayed around them just in time to step off the curb and almost get flattened by a school bus full of kids. The bus came to a screeching halt, the kids got off, and I watched a handful of them make a beeline past another block full of the same type of human struggle and straightaway into a McDonald's. The rest went across the street into some low-end government housing.

I finally arrived at my destination and was greeted and shut-
tled upstairs to talk to some of our nation's best church leaders.
For two days they talked about how to build their churches, how
to multiply their congregations and develop leaders. I know they
didn't mean to, but little mention was given to real people. It
was like we were looking out the tiny passenger window from a
747 jet and seeing a plane fly by in the other direction; I felt that
somehow we were missing Jesus and human beings amid all this
church stuff.

On the way back to the airport I found myself again in a cab.
I didn't care about the dirty headrest. I was tired and about asleep,
but my mind was being perked and sobered by the cool grooves and
sultry riffs of a song by Jason Mraz. I figured it was about a man's
unconditional pursuit of a girl, but as I looked out the window at
real faces of hurting, lonely humans, I couldn't stop projecting the
lyrics onto the heart of God for people—His people. The song is
called "I Won't Give Up."

"Lupe … can you turn up the radio back here for a second?"

"Yes sir," my new cabbie friend replied, and then I laid my head
back, closed my eyes, and heard the words: "I won't give up on
us, even if the skies get rough, I'm giving you all my love, I'm still
looking up … I won't give up."[1] As the song continued from the
distorted speaker behind my left ear, I found myself wiping back
some tears because I was thinking of a God who left divine utopia
and came into a cesspool of brutal human misery. Why? Because of
people. People matter. You matter. God's reason for coming in the
flesh, or better yet for sending His beloved Son in the flesh, is us.
It's me. It's you.

These next few chapters are all about incarnation: what it was, why it happened, and why we struggle with it. As you read, try not to get lost in the concepts or linger in the stories. At times, shut the book and stop reading. Sit there and think, pray, write down questions, and rest. The book can wait. Tomorrow, you will wake up and walk as a human in a sea of humanity. Hopefully, you will enter the lives of people in a different way and with a different hope.

1

NOSTALGIC GOD

He Came Because He Wants It the Way It Was

To truly appreciate what Jesus's incarnation means to us, we have to ask the *why*. Why did God come to earth? Why did He go through all the trouble? Why didn't He just forget about humanity, let it go, and start over? Why would He let His Son not only come to us but also die in the process? If you have grown up with Christian theology, you know that a perfect, holy God cannot let imperfection, or what we call "sin," have the last laugh. Because God is in His nature both perfect in love and perfect in justice, He needed a way to remove sin from humanity so that humans could be back in relationship with Him. The only payment, or what we call "atonement," for sin is someone without sin dying in the place of those who do sin. The only option therefore was God's sinless Son in place of us, sinful humanity.

That makes sense at least as an equation for why God had to come and die. But the incarnation isn't just about an equation. It's about an emotion. God wanted us back. He wanted it the way it used to be.

Nostalgia means "to return or go back home." It is an emotion like homesickness.

In my office I have several pictures. One is with my daughter Alli. She is standing with me in the Yellowstone River. Our backs are turned to the camera so you can see a beautifully snowcapped mountain casting reflections on the water as we're both fly-fishing. She was ten. Next to that is a picture of the first bull elk I shot after eight years of unsuccessful attempts. It was the perfect hunt. As a herd of elk came crashing through an opening in some deep, dark timber in the Grand Mesa, I hid inside some scrub oak. All the cow elk came running by my left shoulder, some even grazing my arm. The last elk, the six-by-six herd bull, stopped as it caught my scent. Then it came through, following the herd. I wheeled around and fired from twelve inches away. It dropped immediately, and for thirty minutes I just sat in silence, thinking, *I must be God's favorite human.* Next to that photo is another with both my daughters stooping down in a river that ran beside our vacation cabin. It was our favorite spot, and the photo fills my mind with memories that could sustain me forever. That trip was the best of everything.

We all have nostalgia and memories of going back home. Some of us remember our fathers through old cars; some of us keep Christmas ornaments our mothers passed down. Maybe it's old guns; maybe just a photo. But whatever the point of reference, we all know the emotions of looking back to times that brought us great joy. Nostalgia is the answer to the *why.*

God is not a robot. He isn't a comptroller of an accounting company trying to make things add up or work out. He is a being full of deep emotion, longing, and memories of what it used to be like. The incarnation therefore isn't about an equation but about remembering what home used to be like and making a plan to get back there. Consider this reboot of the Genesis creation account. It may help you see God's emotion a little better.

> First off, nothing … but God. No light, no time, no substance, no matter. Second off, God says the word and WHAP! Stuff everywhere! The cosmos in chaos: no shape, no form, no function—just darkness … total. And floating above it all, God's Holy Spirit, ready to play.

> Day one: Then God's voice booms out, "Lights!" and, from nowhere, light floods the skies and "night" is swept off the scene. God gives it the big thumbs up, calls it "day".

> Day two: God says, "I want a dome—call it 'sky'— right there between the waters above and below." And it happens.

> Day three: God says, "Too much water! We need something to walk on, a huge lump of it—call it 'land'. Let the 'sea' lick its edges." God smiles, says, "Now we've got us some definition. But it's

too plain! It needs colour! Vegetation! Loads of it. A million shades. Now!" And the earth goes wild with trees, bushes, plants, flowers and fungi. "Now give it a growth permit." Seeds appear in every one. "Yesss!" says God.

Day four: "We need a schedule: let's have a 'sun' for the day, a 'moon' for the night; I want 'seasons', 'years'; and give us 'stars', masses of stars—think of a number, add a trillion, then times it by the number of trees and we're getting there: we're talking huge!

Day five: "OK, animals: amoeba, crustaceans, insects, fish, amphibians, reptiles, birds, mammals … I want the whole caboodle teeming with *a million* varieties of each—and let's have some fun with the shapes, sizes, colours, textures!" God tells them all, "You've got a growth permit—use it!" He sits back and smiles, says, "Result!"

Day six: Then God says, "Let's make people—like us, but human, with flesh and blood, skin and bone. Give them the job of caretakers of the vegetation, game wardens of all the animals." So God makes people, like him, but human. He makes male and female…. He smiles at them and gives them their job description: "Make babies! Be parents, grandparents, great-grandparents—fill the earth with your families and run the planet well. You've got all the plants to eat from, so have all the animals—plenty for all. Enjoy." God looks at everything he's made, and says, "Fantastic. I love it!"

Day seven: Job done—the cosmos and the earth complete. God takes a bit of well-earned R&R and just enjoys. He makes an announcement: "Let's keep this day of the week special, a day off—battery-recharge day: Rest Day."[1]

I'm not normally a paraphrase guy, but we always read the creation story like a textbook. I love this rendition because it captures the enthusiastic emotion that God felt about everything He created, especially humans. He loved it all. He loved us. Most of all, He loved the way things were. Life ran perfectly. We were in perfect relationship. We had perfect purpose. Perfect provision. Perfect protection from anything bad. It was even perfect in that we had a choice to keep it that way.

The choice came in a tree that God put in the middle of Paradise. After He gave Adam and Eve the fullness of perfection in every way, He asked them not to eat from this one tree. They did, and *bam*! Just like the herd of elk crashing through the timber, the earth began to groan and crack with noises and screams, lies, shame, guilt, pain, broken dreams, broken relationships—*sin*!

Was God caught off guard? Did the incarnation become a plan B that God had to put into motion? *No.* God knew that His perfect love would require free will to have its day, and He knew what we would choose. As an old song says, "It was not a haphazard event, or a secondary scheme, but it was the plan of the Lord to redeem."[2] God knew as He was creating perfection that He would lose perfection and have to buy us back to get us home. God was nostalgic, and He still is today! His memories seeped vivid, living color; epic smells, sights, and sounds; and experiences with His created friends, animals, streams, forests, and food. And that's why He made plans to send His Son. He wanted to go back to the way it was!

THE BIG BUYBACK

Okay, now that we see God emotionally longing to have creation— and especially us humans—back the way it was, let's dive into a theological word that really colors in the lines. The word is *redemption.*

Redemption sounds lofty, but it just means "to buy back."

Nostalgia born of beautiful memories is the deep emotion that moved God to want to have things the way they were. Redemption was the pathway He created to get back there.

A question many people have in relation to sin is, Why didn't God just forgive everyone and let folks start fresh every day? Why let His Son die if He could just let everything go? Well, the answer is actually simple. If God just forgave sin without fixing sin, then the destruction of Paradise would continue: pain, unfulfilled potential, ruined lives. Essentially the world would run like Mad Max in the Thunderdome because people cannot fix themselves.

Jesus's life, death, and resurrection proved not just that God wanted us back but that He has power over sin and imperfection and that His original design can be renewed, rebuilt, and reconceived.

Don't think of the doctrine of the incarnation as doctrine. The incarnation is a story of passion. God longed for everything to be back the way it was, and therefore He sent His Son, Jesus, to remedy the cycle of sin so that everything could be made new! That is way more than something to be studied. It is something to be considered and reflected on. That is the *why* of incarnation, and if you don't stop to ponder why Jesus came, you will most likely miss the passion God wants to give you for living incarnationally for those around you.

REFUND DENIED

I've had the fortune of knowing quite a few people who have adopted children from other countries. In every case these children are being literally purchased from a life of parentless poverty. You would think that the process would go much easier than it does, but each case is full of lengthy delays, expensive additional fees, and multiple trips before a child is released to his or her new family. And then it gets worse. As children experience this literal "redemption," they often lash out in anger at the loving parents who are trying to give them a new life. The children have to learn a new language, they can't believe they won't be abandoned again, and they'll even fight other siblings for food because they have gotten used to rummaging for daily sustenance. One close friend of mine said, "I never thought it would be so hard to get my adopted son to believe he's actually adopted."

You would think that when people hear about God's love and His plan to send Jesus, they would run full throttle toward this story. No other religion offers a God who pursues humanity. Not one! Other religions paint a picture of gods who sit back and judge, leave us to our own devices, and wait for us to screw up. But faith in Jesus is simply not that. It's faith in a God who became one of us, who came to us and pursues us. But so many reject this faith, and even a large percentage of those inside the ranks never view their faith in context of His full humanity. We settle for faith about Him, and we let Him be our Savior … but so few let Him actually buy their lives back. We love Jesus as a baby on Christmas, and Jesus risen from the grave on Easter, but somehow we miss Jesus the man, the teacher, the sage, the rebel, the subversive King, the local hero, the neighborhood friend. It is in all of these characteristics that He models a way to buy our lives back, to redeem us. But we miss it and settle for worshipping Him and waiting for Him to come back when all the while He offers us a pathway back to Paradise.

As you think about truly letting Jesus live His life in your life, or you living His life, try not to focus so much on reaching others, converting sinners, or challenging the saints. Redemption is a much bigger picture. God wants you to have His life. Jesus said that the whole reason He came was so we might have life—abundant life. He didn't come and take on flesh so that you would someday pray a salvation prayer, go to church, and settle for a semireligious life. He has bigger hopes and dreams for you than that. He came so that His divine life could actually take root in you and so that you could relate to Him like humans used to before sin messed everything up. So don't let the incarnation be just about you helping *others* find God.

First, stop and smell the proverbial roses a bit, and realize that Jesus came for you!

FLESH FOR YOU

Most people I know believe that Jesus came to earth and died for the sins of all humanity. But most do not believe that He came to earth for them or died for them *personally*. When we see God sending His Son, many of us picture God as an angry principal and Jesus as the vice-principal sent down to get the wayward delinquent out of the class for punishment. Somehow when we picture God coming to us, we just think He's ticked off!

Imagine Adam just a few seconds after he screwed up the entire rhythm of humanity. Now, I've messed up a few things in my life. I've made some mistakes that cost me dearly and some that even hurt others. But consider how you would feel if you were Adam, having just brought sin into the world. You just screwed up perfection! That would be the major gaffe!

If that were you, how would you imagine God coming to you? Do you remember hiding under the covers after disobeying your earthly father? I do. In fact, one of my most memorable experiences with my dad came after I had spilled a paint can all over the carpet while my parents were remodeling a room. They didn't see it happen, so I went flying up the stairs and dived under my covers. In a few minutes I could hear the muffled voice of my father discussing how I had ruined the carpet. I tightened the sheet over my head and tried to prop up stuffed animals and pillows so he couldn't find me. I heard him call out to me. Then I heard his feet coming up the stairs.

"Hugh Thomas, where are you?" Trying not to even breathe, I remained silent. Then the door opened with a creak, and I felt his feet moving toward the side of my bed. I was terrified. I knew he had found me. I expected him to grab me by the ankle, jerk me out of the bed, hang me upside down, and whale away on my hind end with a wooden spoon. But he didn't. I just remember him gently grabbing the corner of the sheet, slowing pulling it up, sliding his face under the covers where he could make eye contact with me, and then saying, "Son, you ruined the carpet, but I love you. Why don't you come down and help me fix this? I'm not mad, but we have to clean it up, okay?"

When God came to find Adam, He was upset, for sure. Disappointed? Yep. And grieved to the core. But He came to Adam. He asked Adam some important questions before He addressed his massive misstep. So there goes your Old Testament image of the angry madman. If God didn't spank Adam then, you are probably safe now! Sure, there were some big consequences, like screwing up the entire universe, but there was a way of redemption for Adam and there is a way for everyone to be bought back. The fact that Jesus came, lived among us, and then died for us is proof of our sin and need for a Savior, but it is just as much proof that we are worth saving. For you to live incarnationally, don't move past this point. Jesus came to earth for you.

FLESH FOR THEM

But He also came for *them*. Who's them? Everyone who's not you!

I went to Haiti last year. I had only seen pictures and heard stories of this broken place after an earthquake left over one hundred thousand people dead in an instant. I had to see and feel this for myself. As I had pictured in my mind, Haitians were largely homeless, sitting on the roadsides, rummaging for anything to eat. Because of their desperate situation, many Haitians are not safe to be around. We had a security team constantly moving us from place to place, protecting us. Our driver, a local Haitian, tried to explain his own tension in watching his fellow citizens become savages: "I have known many of these thieves since I was a young man. Many were my closest friends. I see them now in alleyways, waiting to mug, hurt, and steal, but I still love them. I know them, and I know why they are broken."

In an incredible story, the book of Jonah is about God sending Jonah to the equivalent of modern-day Haitians. The Ninevites were known as crazy people, many of whom were killing children, serving false gods, and terrorizing tourists and locals alike. But God was sending someone with hopes of redemption. The rest of this book will be about God sending you just like God sent Jonah and then sent Jesus, and as hard as it is for you to personalize Jesus coming to earth for you, it will be even harder for you to believe that God can use you in the lives of others. Incarnation is going to ask you to see people like my Haitian driver saw other Haitians. Second Corinthians says this: "We no longer view people from a worldly point of view" (5:16, author's paraphrase). This one verse can be your life force. Incarnation is going to ask you to have full faith in God's ability to transcend what you presently see in someone's life.

During the Haitian relief effort, Beyoncé reworked the lyrics of a song called "Halo." The phrase "Haiti, I can see your halo" is exactly what I'm talking about. If you can see a halo over a bombed-out city like Port-au-Prince, you will learn to see a halo above every friend and enemy God leads you to live next to.

FULL REFUND

The final thing I want you to know about redemption is that it is a full refund. God didn't do all this and give His one and only Son for a partial refund or in-store credit. He came to get every penny back. A partial refund looks like a little bit of religion tacked on to normal life. But a full refund means you learning about God's kingdom and how you get to live in it. For now, consider moving past the standard individualistic, consumeristic, churchianity that many of us have settled for. God has opened up His divine life to you, and it's worth reconsidering everything in light of this tangible opportunity.

Christians often make it sound like Jesus came only to die for sin and then make converts, grow a religion called Christianity, and make more converts. But God never wanted converts, church attenders, prisoners, or parishioners. He wanted His family back. In John 17, Jesus was at the end of His fleshly life. He was about to give His Father's master plan of redemption into the hands of eleven knuckleheads He'd spent three years with. They knew a lot, but they'd also missed a lot. As they listened to Him, He started to pray for them, and one of the most astounding lines comes in verse 21: "I pray that they will all be one, just as you and I are one" (NLT). Notice that Jesus didn't pray that they would grow churches or make converts, start nonprofits, or stop sinning. He didn't pray that they would do a ton of miracles, get people's attention, go on speaking tours, start Bible studies, or lead successful evangelism efforts. He prayed that they would be linked into the family of the Father, the Son, and the Holy Spirit. He prayed that every person rippling out from this handful of men would become grafted into the fellowship of the family. The incarnational way of life is not about conversion. It's about adoption. The book of Ephesians strongly implies that Jesus followers are always to be viewed in the context of the family. We are a part of His body, members of God's household, bride and groom. This understanding is so important because if you miss it, you'll head out your door in the name of Jesus and make prisoners instead of priests, converts instead of cousins, and pharisees instead of family members.

Think. Have you ever thought about God pursuing you even today? Why might He still be coming after you? What is He saying to you this week?

Feel. How does it make you feel to think about a God who longs for you and traded in the life of His Son so that every aspect of your life could be redone, renewed, redeemed? Take a moment to consider the broken places of your inner life and wonder how it might feel to have those things put back together.

Do. Since God is still pursuing every person today, think for a moment—are there people you have given up on or written off? Make a list of those people by name, and consider what it might look like for you to have the same longings for people that God does. What can you do for them?

2

SPIRITUAL VERTIGO
Reorienting the Spiritually Disoriented

The smell of a dog's breath and milk holds the deepest of memories.

Rosco is now forty-two years of age. He travels the world, creating powerful documentaries about homelessness, poverty, hunger, and abuse. He's a storyteller and seems drawn to the worst of the worst in hopes that something good may come out of his art.

Roscoe is an atheist. A really benevolent one.

Thirty-seven years ago, at the age of five, Rosco found himself hiding under a table in his family's small Northern Ireland cottage, desperately trying to keep his dog quiet by distracting him with a bowl of milk. He was hiding under the table because his mother, in fear of losing more family members, had scattered the children just seconds before a band of IRA henchmen came in, holding his father at gunpoint.

In that moment, Rosco prayed that God would save his father. The answer? The sound of a pistol discharging, followed by a deadening thud as his father hit the kitchen floor right next to the table. The fading memories of the day God didn't answer, combined with seeing his father's murderer singing hymns and taking Communion in Mass the next week, left Roscoe with no faith in God at all and only the lingering memory of the smell of his dog and the milk.

How do I know Rosco? I just performed a marriage between him and his fiancée, Tanya. I heard this amazing story over coffee at Starbucks before Rosco flew in to Denver. Tanya, a struggling Christian, was trying to give me the context for why she was marrying an atheist. She spoke emotionally about all the Christian men she had dated and how poorly she was treated, how she was lied to, pushed toward sexual sin. "Rosco has been the most gentle, kind, and respectful man I've ever known. I do hope that someday we can grow together spiritually, but I wanted you to know his story, because his story really matters, and I understand it."

COSMIC DILEMMA

Hearing Rosco's tragic experiences, you probably understand why he doesn't think God exists. You may also find yourself sad for him and others like him who have endured religious or spiritual experiences that brought deep internal disorientation. On one hand, you feel frustration because you know things like this happen all the time, but you also wonder how to break through the fog to help people see God differently. You may want to shout from the mountaintops, "But that's not God!" or "God hates that stuff too!" or "But God didn't do that to you!" But you know that the proclamation of truth seldom penetrates the rocky soil of a heart that's been scarred by repulsive religion and the agony of a hard life. How do we help people see God apart from those things that have happened in God's name? How can we, in a few sentences, bring context to a confused conversation someone has been having in his or her own consciousness for twenty-five years? How can each of us, as one person, help our friends reorient after a lifetime of tradition, doctrine, customs, and beliefs picked up from the overwhelming majority around them?

It's a dilemma, isn't it?

Well, that was exactly God's cosmic mess. He longed for people to return to the way of life He had created before sin screwed up everything. He deeply desired for them to come back in a relational sense as sons, daughters, friends, and family members, but He knew that the hardness of heart and the hardness of life would make it impossible for them to see Him clearly or find a clear path back to Him. Sending prophets—or in our vernacular, preaching harder— wouldn't get it done anymore. People had lost their ear for truth and couldn't stomach any more baseless religion. Proclamation had run its course. Incarnation was now His only play.

In John 1:14, we hear the most powerful statement on the incarnation in Scripture: "The Word became flesh and made his dwelling among us. We have seen his glory, the glory of the one and only Son, who came from the Father, full of grace and truth." We will be looking at this verse from a few hundred different angles throughout this book, but for now, I just want you to notice the part about how people saw His glory. God's glory is His essence, His true persona, His unique attributes, and His trueness. Jesus took on flesh so that people could see God as He really is.

SPIRITUAL VERTIGO

In Jesus's day, people were all lumped in categories and given names. Ninevites, Samaritans, heathens, lepers, Gentiles! This is why someone, when told that Jesus might be the Messiah, said, "Can anything good come from Nazareth?" (John 1:46 NLT). As people always have, we use words like *Democrat, Republican, right-wing, left-wing, homosexual, Southern Baptist, charismatic, unchurched, sinner, non-Christian,* or *unbeliever* (we could go on forever) to place people in boxes whereby we can judge the totality of who they are or what they can become. But these generalizations and names only prove our collective vertigo.

People are not pagans to be converted, projects to be preached at, or demographics to be reprogrammed. Humans should never be generalized, categorized, dismissed, judged, or underestimated. Every person is a story, rich with history, experiences, creative potential, strengths and weaknesses, clarity and blindness. And although spiritual vertigo is universal, we must not put everyone in the same box.

Jesus never belittled people who were spiritually disoriented, because He knew the whole context of their spiritual struggle. It's just like when I worked with teenage sex offenders and found, through reading their criminal files, that their abusive behavior to others was triggered by the incredible abuse they themselves had endured. Getting the full story really changes how we view an ugly chapter. Jesus read the files of sinners He walked among. He respected people's unbelief. When speaking of people who were not yet His followers, He called them friends, blind, prisoners, lame, or lost sheep. And those names clearly showed He understood all the barriers and dilemmas and difficulties they would face in finding Him. He was amazingly understanding of their stories and knew that each person was in process.

If you were to talk to many of my non-Christian friends ("unbelievers"), they would say, "I do believe in God." As I have talked with people outside our typical Christian box—many of whom are my best friends—I have found incredible faith in God, deep conviction about morality, and convicting compassion for the poor and oppressed. Often I've felt like the "worst of sinners" when stacking my own life up against theirs. I've come to realize that even if people call themselves atheists, or agnostics, or even believers, they really aren't—at least not completely.

Most people are really trying-to-be-believers. Although Christians live by a belief system, we stop believing all the time. We fail to trust God with our money and our children; we quickly move to frustration with God when things don't work out; we strive and work for the same empty American dream unbelievers do, and on and on and on. We log on to porn sites, file for divorce, and fudge our taxes like everyone else. We are all disoriented or at least have a massive built-in propensity to screw up our lives and see things the wrong way. Knowing this about ourselves helps us have much greater patience for and faith in others.

GETTING THROUGH THE THICKETS

So for now, incarnational living is going to challenge us to view everyone—including ourselves—as at least a little lost. I've heard all the jokes about how men never stop to ask for directions or admit they're lost, and to some extent they are true. Most men would never raise a hand or hoist the white flag, but we do pull in to gas stations on occasion when we are momentarily "unclear" about the fastest route somewhere. Men will pretty much do anything except claim lostness.

Case in point—take my buddy Lou. Lou and I have gone hunting together a few times in the Grand Mesa wilderness area. Most guys go where you can take a four-wheeler or your camper trailer or stay in a hotel to secure a nice warm shower after a rough day of hiking. But not us. Oh no … we're just too stupid. We go where you have to walk four miles just to set up camp. This land is rough, wild, and raw.

Our first year, Lou and I spent a good majority of the time trying to find passable land between huge rock slides and oak thickets. For those of you who have never been in an oak thicket, it's like trying to climb a wall of inch-thick briars. It's almost impassable. Well, this year, Lou was across the canyon from me and apparently got separated from the other guys he was with by just a hundred yards or so. Matt and Mike (more reasonable and conservative fellows) stuck close to the trail but, after waiting quite a while, realized Lou must have missed the main path out. They hiked down and found the spot where Lou's footprints veered off. After a hundred yards or so they noticed that the prints went directly into a thick patch of these thickets. They tried to look for a way through but could find only the very smallest of openings—about the size of a football. They looked around to see if he had bounced in another direction but saw nothing. Guided by curiosity, like Lucy finding a small passageway into Narnia, Matt and Mike dived through and made it only thirty or forty feet. It was just too thick—but Lou's prints kept going!

Later as they were sitting around the fire, the guys asked him, "What were you thinking?" Lou sheepishly said, "I just didn't want to turn back. I was so far in there, and it was so hard getting to the spot, I couldn't conceive of turning around … so I just plowed through." At one point, a limb knocked off his orange hat. It fell only ten feet back. But he was so tired, he just stared at it and decided he didn't have the heart or will to try to save it! After just a few more feet, Lou hit the wall. Literally. The thickets led to a cliff but kept going up. Lou, in frustration, just continued on until he realized he was no longer hiking through thickets but climbing up them. At that point he reached mental clarity: *I am lost!*

Matt got ahold of Lou on the walkie-talkie. "Lou … where are you, man?"

Lou replied, "Matt, I'm in hell!"

The boys eventually got him back to the trail, and as they recovered that night around a warm fire, they laughed at how Lou had entered hell because he missed the trail by just thirty feet.

To be incarnational means you must take the vertigo seriously. You must learn to respect people's lostness; you must become a deep listener and learn to dignify people's spiritual journeys. And when you hear what has happened to them or not happened to them regarding spiritual matters, you must identify with them or put yourself in their shoes so that maybe someday you can help them see Jesus as separate from those bad experiences. You've got to help them see the real face of God.

REVEALING HIS FACE

Jesus came and lived among people to show us the true face of God.

Check out these face-revealing verses:

My goal is that they may be encouraged in heart
and united in love, so that they may have the full
riches of complete understanding, in order that they
may know the mystery of God, namely, Christ, in
whom are hidden all the treasures of wisdom and
knowledge. (Col. 2:2–3)

You can see why the apostle Paul made it his goal that people
would have complete understanding about Jesus. Jesus shows us
exactly who God is! I often tell people that if you really want to
know what God is like—His emotions, His heart for people, what
He thinks about screwball people who live wrong, what He thinks
about religion or evil in the world, or His plan for humanity—all
you have to do is watch Jesus!

Even Jesus said in John 14:9, "Anyone who has seen me has seen
the Father."

Remember, Jesus did not come to convert people. Nowhere did
He ever say that was His goal. What we do see is that His primary
desire was to give glory to the Father by revealing His glory. Jesus
wanted to help us through our vertigo and give us as clear a picture
of God as He could. I wonder if Jesus wants us to have the same goal.

BACK TO ROSCO

Even with my limited knowledge of Rosco's story, I knew that Jesus
was asking me to become a bit fleshier to him. What I knew was
that Rosco was Irish, that he had experienced only negative feelings
and emotions in regard to religious leaders and systems, and that

he needed to see something of God without all the stereotypes he expected.

The place where Rosco and Tanya's wedding ceremony was held was a sixty-acre Seventh-Day Adventist residence, complete with a private chapel. Seventh-Day Adventists don't allow alcohol in any context, even a wedding. But forbidding alcohol to an Irishman is insensitive enough—even worse not to allow malted barley beverages at a wedding ceremony.

So I simply did what Jesus did at the wedding in Cana: I honored the marriage. I called Rosco out to my Jeep, drove him a half mile down the long driveway, and parked outside the private gate. I then reached into the glove box and pulled out two small shot-size Jameson whiskey containers. As soon as Rosco saw the bottles, he whispered, "No way." I smiled and began to crack open both of them. With the beginnings of tears in his eyes, he said, "I thought you were a pastor."

"I am," I replied.

"Are you sure this is okay?" he asked.

"Well, it's obviously not okay to the owner of this wedding chapel, but I follow Jesus, and He got His initial headline billing because He turned hundreds of gallons of water into wine at a friend's wedding, so I don't think He'll mind if you and I enjoy a quick nip of Ireland's finest."

I continued, "Rosco, Tanya told me a little about your story. I understand why you have had a hard time believing in God. I want you to know that I hope someday you can wipe away the images of religious hypocrisy, rules, and traditions that might have kept you from seeing the real God."

As the conversation ended we both toasted. I shared a quick blessing and prayer over him, and he offered an Irish blessing over me. His was actually better! It was a good moment, a God moment, and Rosco knew that his story mattered to me and to God.

Think. Can you identify the people, things, or experiences that have disoriented you spiritually? Make a list of the biggies.

Feel. In all those situations or with any of those people, can you see God apart from them? In other words, are you blaming God for things that He's not responsible for?

Do. Have you taken time to listen to the unique spiritual stories of the people around you? If not, whom might you schedule a coffee time with? Don't make it weird; just say, "I thought about you today, and I'd love to sit down and hear more about your story."

3

A NEW GOSPEL

What He Came to Say and Bring

What's the worst good news you've ever received? Here are a few that come to mind for me.

"Mr. Halter, this is Bill from the Ford service department. I've got some good news for you. All the smoke you saw wasn't from a blown head gasket. It was actually from your transmission. The cost is only going to be $3,500 to fix it instead of $4,500." *Oh yeah!*

Once, my neighbor Steve called me while I was picking up my daughter from school: "Hugh, I think the salmon you had on the grill is done."

"Why do you say that, Steve?"

"Well, I can see huge plumes of smoke billowing off of the cedar wall you built around your barbecue. I think your entire house may be on fire too!" *Okay, thanks for calling me instead of saving my house, you jackwagon!*

Just after frantically waking up from an unplanned nap in terminal A, gate 43, and noticing that no one but me was still in the seating area, I heard these words from the ticket agent: "Well, sir ... I've got good news and bad news. You did sleep through the boarding process, but you can now go back to sleep and relax for another seven hours before the next flight leaves." *Argh!*

I'm sure you've had a few of these yourself. Seems like bad news usually trumps good news, doesn't it? And thus, most of us feel some level of skepticism when people tell us that they have "good news."

I bring this up because many of us have come to believe in what is called the gospel. The gospel is viewed as a noun that represents the main story about Christ's death, burial, and resurrection and as such has become the main message that Christians believe we should get out to the world. I say *noun* because we view it as this thing that is self-contained, simple, and packaged in a nice, neat wrapper. We preach the gospel, we write books about the gospel, and we even try to get people to go tell random strangers about the gospel. But somehow our fervency to share it—and others' receptivity to it—is dropping like a sack of russet potatoes out a five-story building. We are taught that "gospel" is the main thing, yet most Christians go their entire lives without telling even one friend about it—and even when we do, the response isn't that impressive. So what gives?

Maybe we have a gospel problem. Maybe our good news has become bad news.

The word *gospel* literally means "good news." Based on that simple definition, you'd think that the Christian movement would be growing like moss on a wet rock. In a world full of pressure, strife, poverty, abuse, fiscal cliffs, Haitian earthquakes, pedophile priests, and school shootings, who seriously doesn't like a little good news breaking into this bad-news world? It's impossible not to want good news as long as it's really good news.

THE BAD NEWS ABOUT THE GOOD NEWS

In Galatians 1:6–9, Paul talks about getting the gospel wrong. Or to put it another way, he's trying to help us keep the bad news out of the good news:

> I am astonished that you are so quickly deserting the one who called you to live in the grace of Christ and are turning to a different gospel—which is really no gospel at all. Evidently some people are throwing you into confusion and are trying to pervert the gospel of Christ. But even if we or an angel from heaven should preach a gospel other than the one we preached to you, let them be under God's curse! As we have already said, so now I say again: If anybody is preaching to you a gospel other than what you accepted, let them be under God's curse!

Why is Paul so hot under the collar? Well, because God is. God hates it when people call something good news when it's bad news. Paul doesn't want the gospel being disguised in religious legalism, empty ritual, or personal judgment—which, by the way, are the three things most non-Christian people think our gospel is all about!

Imagine you are a first-century non-Jewish person hearing the gospel for the first time. It might sound something like this: "Okay, you can be a part of God's people, but you have to be circumcised and also stop eating certain meats like pork." How in the north suburb of hades is that good news? Imagine trying to talk your friends into being a Christ follower and waxing on for an hour about sin and how we all have it but that Jesus died for us and will accept us so that no matter what we've done, we can be born-again and live eternally. And then at minute sixty-one, your buddy Billy Bob says, "Yeah, it sounds pretty good. I think I'd be an idiot not to buy into that, but before I pull the lever and accept your gospel, are there any hidden strings or red flags I should know about?"

You reply, "Well, just a few small ones, but compared to all the bennies you get, they are sort of nonissues."

"Oh, cool. What are they?"

"Well, you have to have your foreskin removed with a sharp flint knife, and you can't have bacon anymore. Aren't you happy I shared the good news with you?"

"Heck no!" That would be my response and the response of just about every red-blooded, bacon-eating man I know. That's a bait and switch. That's not really good news at all. That's lousy news!

Here's how people hear our "gospel" today:

God loves you but can't stand you unless you become a Christian. God wants to set you free, but here's a long list of dos and don'ts. God loves the poor but wants you to give your money to rich churches. God loves lost people but wants you to have only Christian friends. God is preparing a beautiful heaven for after this life, but only those who pray a prayer and go to church get to go.

God didn't come to judge but applauds when His people picket abortion clinics or condemn the practice of yoga. God is perfectly loving toward all humans except homosexuals, left-wingers, vegans, unwed mothers, and those who support strict gun laws.

Some of this is tongue in cheek, but you know it's true. Much of our Christian gospel is not the gospel of Jesus. David Kinnaman of Barna Research surveyed American Christians to find out, "Are we more like Jesus or more like the Pharisees in our attitudes and actions?" The culture has voted and said we're more like the Pharisees. This is exactly why Paul and Jesus would say we need a new gospel. If we commit to live the life of incarnation, we must also commit to share, model, and invite people into what will seem like a new gospel to us ... but which was always the gospel to Jesus.

THE GOSPEL OF SOMETHING?

Jesus's very first words about the gospel came in Mark 1:15, where He said, "The kingdom of God is at hand; repent" (ESV). *Repent* means "to turn around." It is a call for people who are walking in one direction to stop on a dime, look up, turn around, and walk the opposite direction. Jesus is not saying, "Make sure you pray a prayer of repentance, start going to church, and wait for Me to come back." He is saying, "You can live a radically different life because there's a new world order that just broke in, so stop walking in the direction you're going, turn 180 degrees, and walk toward Me and life in the kingdom of God."

A huge realization for me was that the gospel isn't so much a noun as a modifier. It's the good news that describes something else.

And that something else is that Jesus brought heaven to earth. From this one understanding we can read the Gospels about the gospel in an entirely new light. Check these out.

- Mark 1:14: "After John was put in prison, Jesus went into Galilee, proclaiming the good news of God."
- Matthew 4:23: "Jesus went throughout Galilee, teaching in their synagogues, proclaiming the good news of the kingdom, and healing every disease and sickness among the people."
- Matthew 24:14: "And this gospel of the kingdom will be preached in the whole world as a testimony to all nations, and then the end will come."

This gospel "of the kingdom" was the main message that Paul, Stephen, Peter, and the early church leaders proclaimed throughout the book of Acts and into the rest of the New Testament (Acts 8:12; 14:22; 19:8; 20:25; 28:23, 31).

A NEW REIGN

A kingdom is just a realm of influence where a king reigns. So when Jesus says that His kingdom is now "at hand," He's saying, "The way it is in My perfect heavenly realm can now show up in the realms you experience every day." Jesus's gospel is not about a cosmic religious apocalypse upon rebellious pagans. His gospel is about a new messianic kingdom where He rules in the spirit of His Father, a kingdom full of joy, grace, freedom, and release from all that ails humanity.

In Luke 4:18–21, Jesus repeated a prophecy about Himself from Isaiah 61:

> "The Spirit of the Lord is on me,
>> because he has anointed me
>> to proclaim good news to the poor.
> He has sent me to proclaim freedom for the
>> prisoners
>> and recovery of sight for the blind,
> to set the oppressed free,
>> to proclaim the year of the Lord's favor."

> Then he rolled up the scroll, gave it back to the attendant and sat down. The eyes of everyone in the synagogue were fastened on him. He began by saying to them, "Today this scripture is fulfilled in your hearing."

The world doesn't like the church's gospel or the gospel of the pop Christian movement, but it does love the gospel of Jesus because His is truly good news! Almost anyone would applaud and hope for the things Jesus talked about. Jesus's gospel includes salvation of our souls, but that's just the starting point. The kingdom of God means that God is making things right: people get help; they have food on the table, protection from enemies, healing for diseases; and they will get a fresh start. The kingdom means that abuses stop, the poor are cared for, and everyone can be accepted into a true community of meaning and substance.

For Jesus, it is about the kingdom of His Father bringing heaven to earth, adopting people into the family of God, calling them sons and daughters and friends. In God's kingdom we are not just people He saves but fellow heirs of all that the King has. We inherit everything, including the privilege of working with Him to see His kingdom win the day. Now that's good news!

ALL THE TOILETS FLUSH IN HEAVEN

Someday, when God's kingdom comes in fullness, no one will be sad, exploited, belittled, held back, or abused. Everyone will be family. No one will be lonely. Everyone will be accepted. Everyone will have a meaningful job without any pressure to perform. No one will be sick, sorry, or hungry. Everyone will be safe, joy filled, and thankful. There will be no political spin, no corruption, and no need for priests, pastors, counselors, or jails. Everyone will be free from sin, free from fear, and free from self. We will no longer have to pray, fight spiritual forces of darkness, or try to reach anyone for Jesus. Everyone will be in, and all the bad guys will be banished forever! Everything will be perfect. We will never have to go to another DMV, and the toilets will always flush. That's a picture of the kingdom in fullness, after Jesus removes the kingdom of this world for the final time.

But as we sit here now, we live in the tension of two kingdoms fighting for who and what will reign. Jesus said, "And from the time John the Baptist began preaching until now, the Kingdom of Heaven has been forcefully advancing, and violent people are attacking it" (NLT).

This gives us a clue that what Jesus said is true. His kingdom is at hand and is therefore accessible, but it won't come without a fight. We can remove people from oppression, fight for those bound by injustice, lift up and support those who need a little hand to move forward, and we can bring healing to the sick and those who have been abused. We can adopt people, help people find jobs, include them in our lives, extend community to them, and forgive them. We can pray and fight the forces of darkness, and we can even fix a few toilets! But it won't just happen. The good news is really good news, and it will show up at any moment you join God in the work.

Beyond the news stories you've heard about the earthquake in Haiti, you probably also know the story of this country just off the coast of Florida. It is one of the poorest places on earth. Eighty-five percent unemployment, dark voodoo witchcraft as the national religion—and now, after the massive earthquake that killed over one hundred thousand people, it seems like a place resistant to God's kingdom and reign.

Not so! I had the opportunity to travel with a band of kingdom friends called Convoy of Hope. This NGO now serves sixty thousand meals a day through school systems that are sanctioned by church leaders. No, the people in Convoy of Hope don't just put Band-Aids on gushing wounds. They are helping local farmers produce crops that in five years' time could support the needs of the entire country. Children who would never go to school come from villages to find hundreds of schools, led by godly kingdom teachers who give thousands of meals, love, warm smiles, and real hope. This is God's kingdom Convoy in action! The gospel is happening all the time, all over the world. It is at hand!

YOUR NEW GOSPEL

I once had a job selling fireworks. It was kind of fun. I would drive around the state of Oregon, assembling fireworks stands and then stocking them full of *boom, boom, pow.* That is until a dry season (hard to imagine in Oregon) caused a statewide fireworks ban. The business, however, didn't close down. We figured that someday the ban would be lifted, and so we kept trying to sell fireworks. As you can imagine, it didn't go well. I found myself pretty uninspired. Okay, totally uninspired. I didn't believe in what I was selling anymore, and even if I did get some sucker to purchase a box, I really didn't think he would get to use them anyway. I had a lousy product no one wanted to buy or should buy.

That's what the old gospel is like. It's just uninspiring, and I totally understand why people minimize its importance in their lives. Church attendance, fear of hell, moral codes, social judgments, privatized-consumerized-suburbanized-nebulized faith. No one wants that. Not even you. But the gospel of Jesus and His kingdom—now that one will sell every time.

The gospel is not news that we can accept Jesus into our lives. The gospel is news that Jesus has accepted us into His life and that we can live His life now. That's the choice of incarnation: not to just be a Christian but to actually receive God's invitation through Christ to be in the eye of the incarnational storm as He brings redemption to the world. That's worth waking up for! Every day is dripping with meaning, every person you meet is under divine renovation, and thus every second is open to kingdom opportunities. That's great news!

That's why Jesus said in Matthew 13:44–46,

> The kingdom of heaven is like treasure hidden in a field, which a man found and covered up. Then in his joy he goes and sells all that he has and buys that field.
>
> Again, the kingdom of heaven is like a merchant in search of fine pearls, who, on finding one pearl of great value, went and sold all that he had and bought it. (ESV)

From this point on in your quest to live incarnationally, commit—like the apostle Paul in Romans 15:20—to preach the gospel where Christ is not known, so that you are not building on someone else's foundation. So don't just tell them the same old bad-news good news. Be a fresh person with a fresh but ancient story of a God who eats, breathes, and lives to bring redemption to humankind.

Jesus was Good News, and He spoke good news. His reality matched His rhetoric. So can yours.

Think. If someone were to ask you, "What is the gospel?" what would you say? How much of your answer would reflect the afterlife, and how much would reflect this life?

Feel. What aspects of Jesus's gospel would be good news to your friends who don't know Christ? Can you imagine how you might feel if someone brought the kingdom of heaven down to your earth?

Do. Write down characteristics of the gospel you received growing up. Circle the items that were good news, and put an *X* through the items that were bad news. Consider writing an apology note to at least one person you might have shared "bad news" with.

4
INCARNATIONAL LIES
The Real Battle

Since our marriage began twenty years ago, Cheryl and I have tried to commit to having coffee together twice a day. The morning cup is simply for waking up together, getting a heads-up on the events of the day, watching our dogs rummage around the yard. I'll tell you about my twenty-four-year-old son, Ryan, in more detail later, but for now, let me simply mention that he has a doozy of an epilepsy condition. Consequently, many of these morning cups have been sipped after only a couple of hours of sleep. And those times when his seizures hit every night for weeks in a row, this cup of dark java was less about savoring and more about survival. Personally, I don't really like the morning cup. I'm an introvert and an ogreish troll when I wake up, so when my extroverted wife wants to communicate, it takes all the discipline in the world for me to perk up. The second cup is usually shared around 4:00 p.m. This time tends to involve recapping the tragedies and triumphs that may have occurred within the Halter family that day. It's the afternoon cup that I most look forward to enjoying. Traditionally, some of our best visions, plans, dreams, and creative ideas have come from this hour. We dream about vacations, Ryan getting better, the lives of our girls, church stuff, what our date might be for the week (okay, the month), and a host of other hopeful opportunities.

As we look back, most of our dreams, in reality, have gone unfulfilled. We're normal peasants, so we get stuck in the mundane reality of our children's schedules, financial constraints, the balancing act of ministry and work, and of course, Ryan's severe disability.

Until the fall of 2011, when finally everything changed.

By sheer Providence we found a 350-person assisted-living ranch for disabled adults. Ryan got accepted into the program and left his ten-by-ten-foot room where he'd essentially spent his entire life.

We are thrilled for him, and candidly we're also pretty excited for *us*!

We can now go on a date without having to box up our food and rush home to scoop his limp body off the floor. We no longer have to say no to our girls if they want to do something with us. We are officially empty nesters, and the options are blowing our minds.

So when Ryan's plans were finalized, I told Cheryl that we should use an afternoon coffee time to plan out our new life together. The day came; we went outside and sat on our front porch, and I said, "Hey, babe, my plan is that in a year, you and I will take that trip of a lifetime. I want to take a six-month sabbatical. We'll start off with three weeks watching the Tour de France, in France, then Chunnel over to England, then zip up to Scotland for the British Open. When we get home, I'll start building that log cabin from scratch!" I was undeterred by Cheryl's somewhat skeptical look, so I continued. "And I'm going to finally take those bagpipe lessons, and then you can go skydiving, Rocky Mountain climbing, and even ride a bull named Fu Manchu!" She wasn't impressed by my ability to link a nice country western song to my plans for our future.

All I heard was the long, drawn-out slurp as she slowly sipped her vanilla crème coffee. Then she said, "You know, before we plan all this, maybe we should pray about our future."

Without thinking, I blurted out, "Heck no! I ain't praying about it. I don't want God to screw up our only chance at a break, some fun, some frolicking and lack of responsibility! We've put in our time, and God can go use some other people for a while!" Cheryl just rolled her eyes while I kept venting. "If we ask His opinion again, He'd probably have us move to the Congo and start an orphanage or make us go back into youth ministry, or even worse, you'll get pregnant and we'll have to start all over again!"

Cheryl finally spoke. "I'd love to be able to take a few weeks off and do the Tour de France; that would be a dream come true. But now we have time to really help people. We could open our house with homeless teens, or even consider an orphanage type of scenario."

"Drat, I knew it!" was my response.

YOU DON'T HAVE TO DO THIS!

Isn't it amazing how when given the option to avoid more mess, trouble, struggle, or responsibility, we usually take it? I mean, heck, life's tough these days. The culture doesn't give us a sacred day off anymore. We keep busy with soccer eight nights of the week, then tournaments on the weekends. The price of gas has us taking on one of those "work from home" jobs where we try to sell energy supplements to our friends. And then we hear that we should be really committed to this thing called church and living a missional life, which supposedly means I have to go try to reach out to my friends, who are actually busier than I am, and *blah blah*.

Are you kidding? Most of us just need a break! One of my friends even shared a brilliant secret he and his wife figured out. They have discovered that you can have date nights simply by dropping off your kids at any local megachurch and then busting off to see a quick movie or grab a bite to eat. I told him, "That's terrible." He said, "Yeah, I kind of feel bad, but dang, what's a church for if it isn't about helping people get a break from their kids?" I have to admit, I was impressed by his resourcefulness.

Look, from the beginning of time, there's been a little voice in our heads that whispers or megaphones us this message: "Pssst. You don't really need to be incarnational. You actually don't have time, and it won't work anyway. So just go back to your own life and try to survive yourself."

You would assume that only demonic forces would be behind such lies, but sometimes the voices come from within our own heads, and from within our Christian community. Read this quote someone sent to me, and see if you can pick up on the subtle misunderstandings that lead people away from incarnation and from taking on the incarnational lifestyle Cheryl was pushing for.

> I have a slight issue with the term *incarnational*. I
> understand and appreciate the impulse to see that

our hands and feet, eyes and tongues, do and live and put on our creed. Yet it's important for us to recognize that, historically, the term *incarnation* has referred to the unique, once-in-history event of God becoming man. No, the term is not a biblical one, but there are good reasons to preserve the uniqueness of the term in our usage. First of all, equating what the divine Son did in becoming Jesus the God-man with what I do when I imitate Jesus downplays the ineffable wonder of that onetime event. It might even be said to make the divine Son a little smaller and me a little bigger. More significantly, the primary purpose of the incarnation, I believe, was for the Son to offer His life as the perfect sacrificial substitute in order to assuage the wrath of God against eternally damnable transgression. Yet when I make the incarnation primarily about something else, something that I can emulate in my own life, I risk shifting the focus away from Christ's wondrous, astounding, amazing work of wrath removal.

This national ministry leader is right to make the focus of the incarnation Jesus and His wonderful sacrifice. And he's correct again that only Jesus could have come to die for the sins of humanity. The atonement of Jesus, His paying for the sins of humanity, is the single most important game changer in the history of the universe. Without Jesus's sacrifice for sin, every person would be stuck in it and ultimately die in sin. So *yes*, Jesus came to die for sin and sinners, but that is not the only reason He came to earth.

Jesus also came to live a life. He came to model a new way to be human. He came in the flesh to show us how to live in our flesh. And this is where this fella and so many miss the full meaning of the incarnation. We miss the incarnation when we view Jesus only through His death on the cross instead of through His life in the neighborhood.

IT AIN'T ALL ABOUT THE CROSS

Do you know what the earliest Christian symbol was? You probably guessed the cross, right? Nope. The cross became a well-known symbol about three hundred years after Jesus as the Roman Empire conquered countries and kingdoms in the name of Jesus. Before that, the main symbol was an anchor. Why an anchor? It was because God's people, the true Jesus followers, were constantly on the run, on mission, in trouble, in prayer, building community, experiencing sacrifice and loss—and they were in need of a symbol that reminded them that they were safe and secure. While the symbol of the cross became and still remains a symbol that focuses on what Jesus did for us, the anchor is a symbol of what He is for us while we live for Him. The anchor is a symbol of a *sent* people. It really doesn't cost anything to wear a cross. But if you see the cross not only as what Jesus did for you but also as what He now allows you to be a part of, you're going to need an anchor!

> If you claim to be in Him, you must learn to walk
> as Jesus walked. (1 John 2:6, author's paraphrase)

In this verse, John is calling us past the cross and back into the hood. He is saying that because Jesus died for our sins, we're now free to live like Him! And if we claim to be Christians, the way we bring glory to Him is to model our lives after His life. Our attempt at incarnational life doesn't steal glory from God; it amplifies it!

SUBTLE TEMPTATIONS

As you consider Jesus in the flesh, remember that He had at least one moment when He was tempted by the lies of incarnation and considered getting out of it too. As we read in Matthew 4:1–11, Jesus was in the desert for forty days without food. He was starving, literally. He was weak and vulnerable, and that's when Satan came to tempt Him away from His incarnational mission.

The first lie was aimed at His appetite. There is no temptation stronger than the urge to eat, survive, and fill ourselves. After forty days, wouldn't you find it easy to justify turning a rock or two into a nice loaf of bread? The lies and justification would sound a little like this:

> If I don't take care of myself first, how will I have any energy to help others?
> If I give time or help to those people, surely they will latch onto my life and keep draining me for more.
> I'm still trying to work through my own issues and struggles, so I'd better not try to help another person right now.

> I know we need to include unbelievers in our
> Christian community, but I just need a time
> when I can go deep with other believers.

All these lies hit deeply at our consumerism, that unconscious but ever-present pull to get as much out of Jesus for ourselves as possible without any outflow to others. How did Jesus respond in His legitimate hunger? He set His jaw and told Satan that living with guts is better than living with a full belly. Jesus calls us to let God's mission sustain and satisfy us more than our natural appetites. We don't live to take care of ourselves. We trust God to give us everything we need as we live for others. Jesus invites us to "seek first the kingdom of God and his righteousness, and all these things will be added to you" (Matt. 6:33 ESV).

The second lie is that God will always bail us out if we serve Him. Satan took Jesus to a high point, most likely the top of the temple in Jerusalem. There he quoted part of Psalm 91: "He will command his angels concerning you, and they will lift you up in their hands, so that you will not strike your foot against a stone" (Matt. 4:6). In that moment, Satan had Jesus positioned at the top of the religious world and offered Him the lie that the angels would never let Him fall to His death on the streets where the peasants walked.

The lies of hiding behind religion sound like this:

> If God is in this, He will provide for and protect
> me and my family.
> I've tried to do ministry for God, and it didn't work
> out very well, so I'm not taking that risk again.

> Other Jesus followers don't live incarnationally
> and they seem fine, so I'd just rather be like
> them than go the extra mile.

Looking back on twenty years of living by faith and leading my own family into the mission of God, I've come to one conclusion. Living the gospel costs! If you follow Jesus, you will lose energy, time, money, friends, and quite possibly even more. Last year, my daughter McKenna was assaulted by a boy in her high school. She was trying to break up a fight between him and his girlfriend, who happened to be her best friend. The boy turned on my daughter and slammed her head against a car. This was just two months after her doctor told her that if she had any more blows to the head, she would have to quit playing hockey. Because she came to the rescue, she lost a hockey scholarship, and a year later she is still not completely back to her vibrant self. Of course I tried to find this boy and remove him and his family from the universe. In my rage, I called McKenna and asked her to tell me where he lived, but she wouldn't give me his address. She told me to come home, and then, as I sat on her bed, she said, "Dad, you always taught me to be a peacemaker. Do you actually think that will always work out without any pain?" Through my own tears, I was deeply proud of the woman she had become, but the gut check was more real than I wanted it to be!

In Hebrews 12:1, we are encouraged to keep going with these words: "Therefore, since we are surrounded by such a great cloud of witnesses, let us throw off everything that hinders." Who is in this great cloud of witnesses watching us live? No, it isn't the rich, the well-respected, or those who had visible success at ministry ventures.

Instead, it is a privileged group of faithful saints who lost a lot for serving Jesus. It was and is a countless multitude of humans who died thinking they had failed for God.

I don't know how many times I've sat across the coffee table from people, trying to encourage them to stay in the game with Jesus. After being mistreated in a church or by another Christian, or having a ministry venture fail, most people tend to blame God, get jaded, and find it emotionally draining to pick up the pieces and keep going. But I've found that the only way to encourage people forward is to let them know about the joyful day when they will get to share their story with others who have been through the wringer for God. Imagine the day you find yourself in heaven, sitting in a recovery circle with Abraham, Moses, Rahab, Peter, Paul, and Jesus, and one by one, you get to show your scars and tell the story of all the things you did for God that didn't work. What a badge of honor our failed exploits will be then! What makes the stories of our lives beautiful are not the people we've led to faith, or the churches we've grown, or the poor and hurting people we've renovated. What makes our stories matter are the day-by-day swan dives we take for the King of glory that may never look that glorious—but to God they are! Jesus answered Satan in Matthew 4: "It is also written: 'Do not put the Lord your God to the test'" (v. 7). That wasn't just a statement of rebuke to Satan. It was the word of a man who knew that incarnation calls you to fall to the floor of humanity and die because those who intentionally choose the path of incarnation instead of self-preservation will see God's glory.

The third lie is about real influence versus fake influence. Satan took Jesus to a mountaintop and offered to consolidate the whole world under His command without any work. In a sense, he was giving Jesus the opportunity to have worldwide influence at the flick of a switch. This wasn't the only time Jesus had to fight the natural temptation to take shortcuts and elevate His ministry. After He had fed thousands of people, He had quite a following. In John 6:14–15, we see this: "After the people saw the sign Jesus performed, they began to say, 'Surely this is the Prophet who is to come into the world.' Jesus, knowing that they intended to come and make him king by force, withdrew again to a mountain by himself."

Everyone wants to have influence. We count Facebook fans, Google circles, and Twitter followers. We measure Sunday church attendance and yearly budget numbers, all the while thinking we are creating our own wave. The multitude that followed Jesus was more than willing to speed up His influence and make Him the leader they wanted. But Jesus knew that real influence could be gained only as people were made into disciples one by one.

When Jesus winked at Satan's ploy and said, "Away from me, Satan! For it is written: 'Worship the Lord your God, and serve him only'" (Matt. 4:10), He was saying no to the shortcuts and surface-level leadership and saying yes to a life committed to walking with a few. Whereas Satan tried to use the mountaintop to give Jesus the whole world, Jesus went back to the mountaintop to get away from the world.

When you boil the lies of incarnation down to one simple idea, you find this: Satan could not stop the cross from happening. He has never been able to keep people from being set free in Jesus. But he has been pretty effective at getting people to listen to lies that keep them from going beyond the cross. And although Satan and his minions don't like anyone to acknowledge Jesus as his or her Savior, they will settle for that as long as you don't make Jesus your Lord.

YOU ARE *SENT* LIKE JESUS

Wherever I go, the biggest concern for living incarnationally is about time: "Hugh, I get this, and I know I should be more intentional about all this, but I'm just so swamped I can't imagine having any consistent time or energy for people." My response is always the same: "Anyone has time to be a part-time missionary."

A missionary is just a "sent one." And the story of God sending people to bring hope to the world didn't begin or end with Jesus. When Noah and his family needed hope for a new life, God sent an olive branch. When God's people were hungry in the desert, He sent manna as daily food. When the Israelites were surrounded and held in bondage by enemies, He sent plagues and pestilence and even death to get them out! When their cities and lives were broken because of their disobedience, He sent prophets. And then, in a final play to bring in all the chips, He sent Jesus to earth. As Jesus fulfilled His mission, He busted the lies of the Enemy and the apathy of humanity with these words: "As the Father has sent me, I am sending you" (John 20:21).

So how can any person be at least a part-time missionary? You just have to see everywhere you are as a mission field. For instance, most parents who have kids in school or athletics are on the same set of bleachers with the same parents of the same kids for at least two to three times a week, if not more. There's ten hours of missionary time. If you're a student, you're walking the hallways or enjoying extracurricular activity with people at least five hours a week. Studying together is another ten-hour-a-week opportunity. We also frequent the same coffee shops or pubs on the way to and from work or school, so there's another two to five hours a week on that mission field. Then of course there is the street we live on. Obviously we can't consider all the time we spend in our home missionary time, but if you bring the barbecue from the backyard to the side yard and look for a normal amount of interaction, you will find another five hours of good missionary time right where you live. So there's a simple twenty-hour workweek for any normal American. It can be done if you let God send you.

God has never been the type to send doctrine or pat, easy answers to get us out of conversations. He doesn't send us pastors to do all the work for us or church buildings to keep us safe from doing His work. His longing was and is too deep. He has always sent what we need to help orient us back to Him, and the life of incarnation will always and only happen when we let God send us to the people He longs for us to help. Because God cares for Joe, He will send Steve. Because He loves Lacy, He will send Sarah. Will you let Him send you?

Cast off the lies, and live the life Jesus would live!

Think. Which of the three lies has the strongest grip on you?

Feel. Fill in these sentences.

> When I think about really living incarnationally,
> I'm most afraid of _____.

When I think about really living incarnationally,
        I'm most excited and hopeful about _____.

Do. Show your scars. Make a list of all the things you've done for God that failed. Take some time to reconsider how you feel about them. Keep these in a "Swan Dive File," and throw yourself a party or take yourself out for ice cream to thank God for letting you give a few pounds of flesh on His behalf.

REPUTATION

True story. It was 1:00 a.m. I was doing what I normally do at that time—sleeping next to Cheryl in our upstairs bedroom. Suddenly breaking through my REM sleep was the faint but growing sound of two men talking in our hallway, right outside the open door. Still slightly dazed, I reached over and tapped Cheryl and said, "Can you go see what they want?" Then as soon as I realized the ridiculousness of my less-than-Braveheart-like response, I staggered toward the voices.

Unconcerned about what I was wearing (not much) or the fact that I was heading toward two men in the dark with only my bad breath as a weapon, I confronted the intruders.

"Hugh ... don't shoot; it's Chris and Matt."

As Cheryl joined us in the hallway, Chris continued, "Sorry about breaking into your house, but apparently Alli [my older daughter, who had just gone off to college] is in trouble. She's stuck in a cornfield and doesn't know where she is, and she's freaking out. She called McKenna [my younger daughter, whom I'm not going to let go to college!], and McKenna is now freaking out and called us so we could come tell you!"

Cheryl and I were now wide awake! I was trying to stay calm, but my daddy instincts were kicking into DEFCON 1 as my mind flooded with images of Freddy Krueger from high school horror flicks wielding his switchblade scissor fingers, chasing my screaming, disoriented daughter through a corn maze!

Fortunately, the real story wasn't nearly as dramatic as we thought, and a day later, while Chris and I were riding in my truck, I asked, "Why did you guys sneak in through the garage? Why didn't you just ring the doorbell? Your entry could have gotten you killed!"

Chris scrunched his lips together, got a confused look on his face, and said, "I don't know. Good question."

THE WRONG WAY TO ENTER

Whether it's how a guy offers a ring to his future wife, how a French chef delicately plates an expensive dish, or how a fly fisherman softly lofts a hand-tied caddis fly into a Montana stream, presentation is everything. This next section—"Reputation"—will help us see the brilliant way Jesus entered humanity and lived among people. Jesus may have had some enemies, but the people on the street loved Him. He was the perfect human, a native in the best sense. He built a reputation by how He worked a job, partied with the locals, opened up everyone's homes, and busted through religious and social barriers. He fought for things people cared about and was the most holy but least judgmental person the world had ever seen. A true iconoclast, or "image breaker." As such, His life was much more than a few years lived before the cross. His life is a model for how we can live now.

These next few chapters should help you develop the good "street cred" He had. You will find that your normal, mundane life is perfectly suited to bring glory to God and get people talking.

Incarnation should always lead to a great reputation.

5

BABY/BOY/BLOKE
Becoming Human

I love to people watch. I travel almost every week, so I am blessed to spend countless hours in airports and airplanes. My favorite pastime is to observe the daily patterns of the creatures called humans. One thing I've noticed is that if people think they are being watched, they generally make sure to appear presentable. They will straighten their postures, mind their manners, and try to keep their emotions in check. On the descent, women usually take out their makeup bags to reapply, parents who are obviously getting angry at their misbehaving children strain to keep their voices down, and lovebirds refrain from going overboard with their public displays of affection.

But when humans forget they are being watched, you get a totally different picture.

The angry parent sometimes loses it in the middle of the airport and, with veins popping out and teeth clenched, will grab a two-year-old by one arm, swinging the minihuman around like a tetherball, and then scream, "DangitJoeyknockitoff!" The same woman who a second before was putting on lipstick in the waiting area sometimes ends up sitting next to me on the plane and within ten minutes is fast asleep, head flopping around, jaw relaxed, a four-inch string of drool stretching out of her wide-open mouth. When humans do what is natural, they pick their noses and their teeth and look at their reflections in a window as if none of the forty other people around are watching them admire themselves. Humanity is hilarious!

As we consider incarnational life, I thought it would be fun to take a chapter to talk about being ... a human being. We'll get to us in a moment, but the jaw-dropper is that God became one of us! We love to view Jesus's short-term mission to earth like we might picture a famous athlete shaking hands with the lowly fans or a medieval king leaving his ornate throne to enjoy a brief appearance on the streets with the peasants. But we resist acknowledging that Jesus was actually one of us and that taking on flesh meant that He actually became a real human.

People have always struggled with this because we can't understand how a divine being so perfect can take on the form of us humans, who are always so imperfect. We also have a hard time trying to figure out what we should be since He came to be like us. Should we try to be more godlike? Should we totally deny our humanness or play it down, act more religious? Or what? It is an awkward dance. Some people have said that Jesus became like us so that we can become like Him, and although it may sound nice, it really isn't why He came. He had no intention of trying to get us to be like God, or to be perfect, or to be less human. He actually came to teach us how a true human is to live. And this one shift in understanding will set you free from some false and harmful beliefs that have locked up the church and its people for eons. We'll unpack this a little, but here's the nugget: God doesn't want you to deny your humanity, nor does He want you to try to be more godlike. He came to show you how to live fully human in the way that He did and in a way that you will truly love. But for you to get this, you have to let Jesus be truly human too.

WATCHING JESUS

Can you picture Jesus smashing His finger, biting His lip, dropping to one knee, and wincing in painful laughter? Can you see Him waking up in the morning, heading to the facilities (likely an olive tree), and looking around to make sure no one was watching? Can you imagine Jesus with gas after a bad meal of hummus and sardines? Reflect on Him freezing cold, huddling next to His brothers or mother to try to stay warm. It's easy to picture Him as a baby, but what about as an awkward teenager with raging hormones? What about a twenty-eight-year-old virgin who was maybe one of the last single men in his small village? Can you see Him working long days with His father, going home exhausted, falling asleep, and then waking with a sore neck and swollen fingers?

If not, it will be hard to relate to Him and even harder to live like Him. If you see Him only as God, you may worship Him or study Him, but you will miss the joy of emulating Him.

Jesus was born; He messed His pants; He grew up, hit puberty, got sick, puked, got tired, woke up disoriented, sneezed, scratched his armpits; and yes, Jesus pooped. He got hungry and thirsty and hurt

Himself while playing and working. As He grew, He was curious about life and spiritual matters and was always asking questions. His voice, body, and personality all changed. We know that during His ministry, He got sad, angry, frustrated, and fearful. He laughed, He cried, He fought temptation of every kind, and He experienced physical death. In His birth, He was vulnerable. In His boyhood, He was playful and inquisitive. And as a full-grown manly man, He was the guy next door, a real rustic hombre. He gets the awkwardness of not living like God, so we can relax, put away our goofy attempts to be more godly, and reconsider being truly human.

GODLINESS IS NOT ABOUT TRYING TO BE GOD

I know what you're thinking: *Hugh, but we humans have no shot at making our humanness like that of Jesus. Aren't we totally depraved, desperately wicked, and far from God, as Scripture says? And if this is so, shouldn't we try to become less human and a bit more spiritual, a bit more godly?* Well, not exactly. Second Timothy 3:5 helps us understand this dilemma. Regarding people who were professing faith, standing up for God and the church, and living religiously, Paul said, "They have a form of godliness but deny the power thereof" (author's paraphrase). Jesus taught the same thing when He referred to the uber-religious Pharisees, calling them whitewashed sepulchres and saying that while they looked okay on the outside, they were full of death on the inside (Matt. 23:27). Jesus was teaching that godliness is not about trying to hide our humanness and appear more like God. That always comes off smelling like inauthenticity and reeks of hypocrisy—and neither God nor the observing world buys it. Worse, it doesn't work anyway. Trying to be godly is like trying to be a pro athlete with Parkinson's disease or trying to be as gorgeous as a model in *GQ* magazine when you look like Hugh Halter. It simply doesn't work. Have you ever tried to make it just one day without an angry or lustful thought, selfish act, or second of worry? If you're like me, you may make it only a few hours at best.

And then each Sunday we feel bad, beg for forgiveness, and start the brutal dance of failure all over again. And if we do that long enough, we settle into this "form of godliness" that has no real power. When we deny our humanity and try to become more clean, or more pure, or more *sanctified*, we end up on the wrong end of that word. The word instead becomes *sanctimonious*, and it means we hide our true human struggle and become self-righteous, smug, holier-than-thou, pious, pompous, and a few other lovely terms that describe humans trying to appear more godly than people around them.

For instance, many Christians base their personal sanctification scorecard on whether they had a devotional time that day, avoided swearing, and went to church. But while they may feel great about their "walk with God," they have not loved their neighbors as much as they love themselves, they haven't cared for or even looked to take care of the needs of the sick or the poor, and there's been no focus or intention toward unbelievers in their lives. They may feel clean or pure or godly, but by their lives, they completely deny the power of God. On the other hand, there are many other people who swear and sometimes don't get their devotional time in but who wake up and spend their entire day doing the very works of God in the world. They throw parties for their friends, they take a few hours and help with practical needs, or they spend time with people whom most of the world would never touch. Which do you think Jesus prefers?

In Matthew 3:7, John the Baptist called a spade a spade and called the spiritually elite a basket of snakes. These people put the focus of their lives on outward cleansing all the time, waiting for the Messiah to come back, as many self-righteous Christians do today. John then called them and anyone within earshot to "bear fruit in keeping with repentance" (v. 8 ESV). In other words, stop worrying about your outward spiritual appearance. Stop micromanaging the old scorecard that the religious elite have put before you in the past. Stop trying to manage your sins.

Bottom line, Jesus's payment on the cross for your sin made you holy, righteous, and sanctified. He did it all. You don't get to claim any of it, but you do get to humbly work with God to display His work in your life. First Thessalonians 5:23 says, "May God himself, the God of peace, *sanctify* you through and through. May your whole spirit, soul and body be kept blameless at the coming of our Lord Jesus Christ." Yes, it is God's desire that you grow in the fruits of righteousness and that you take your human imperfection seriously, but don't think for a minute that you can fix yourself. God has made you clean through the perfection of Jesus, so keep your sense of humor about your humanness, and focus instead on the good, the fun, and the meaningful things life in His kingdom has to offer.

Incarnational living isn't about trying to deny our humanness and appear godly. It is about humbly walking among our friends and letting them see how God is changing our humanness.

Thus, to be incarnational and live an incarnational life, you've got to settle the issue of your identity in Jesus. You are His, and every part of your life is under redemptive renovation. Yes, your sinful life, if left unredeemed, will cause every area of your life to be depraved— but you as a person are not totally depraved. You were created or designed in God's image, you *are* redeemed, and your sin *is* removed; thus, your life will always reflect some of the glorious work of God. As Psalm 139:14 says, you are "fearfully and wonderfully made." That means your general design is awesome! Let's start there.

So don't hide your humanness or leave the playing field because you don't feel you've got it all figured out. The more Jesus lives in and through you, the better the reflection; so start right where you are. Start with who you are.

LOOKING CLOSER AT A BEAUTIFUL WOMAN

Pornography is rampant. People think it's normal and just an ugly part of human existence. Unless you're a father of two daughters, as I am. As a pastor I've tried to help countless hundreds of men fight this battle, and after many years I've come to the conclusion that there's only one way to keep a man from looking lustfully at a woman. No, it doesn't work to use the age-old philosophy of trying to get men to deny their humanity or to vilify their sensual or "natural" lusts. To say, "God hates it," when you take a second look at a woman who passes by or to say we are animals with debased passions just never seemed true. There's just too much evidence that God created us with these natural desires. So what answer seems to work? I tell men to look more closely at a woman they are lusting after. What? Yes, stop denying that you are attracted and stop feeling guilty that you are attracted. Instead look more deeply at this woman. Stare at her longer, and while you do, consider these facts. She is a daughter to someone. She has dreams just like you; she has fears just like you; she desires to be valued and cared for—and all over the world, millions of women just like her are abused, raped, and exploited because men settle for base animal lust over redeemed human identity.

Jesus came into our humanity to show us how the original design was meant to be. He taught us how to love a sinner and how to treat the sick and the poor. He showed us the importance of true Sabbath rest, how to work with integrity, and how to be a person of hilarious celebration. He encouraged us to be incredible neighbors and above all to be people who love other people, especially those of the opposite sex. In short, He challenged us not to look away from the computer screen, TV, billboard ad, or lovely woman walking down the street. He actually taught us to look more deeply at other humans. To see God's divine thumbprint alongside the other person's marred human frailty and vulnerability. I challenge any man who looks lustfully at a woman to look a little longer, and while you look, pray for that girl and see if you don't see her differently. You will see everyone differently. We are fathers, sons, or brothers … or we are predators. The difference lies completely in whether we see God's true and original design when we look at other humans. Again, this is why, according to 2 Corinthians 5:16, "from now on, therefore, we regard no one according to the flesh. Even though we once regarded Christ according to the flesh, we regard him thus no longer" (ESV). We must see Jesus as both human and divine. We must see ourselves and every other person as human in context of God's divine work in our lives.

Here are a few critical ways we can become more human like Jesus.

WHIMSICALLY HOLY VERSUS RELIGIOUS

Holiness is an attribute of God that gets applied to us when we place our faith in Jesus. God sees us through the perfection of Jesus, and Jesus's perfection covers our sin. Holiness is also something that we can grow in. We cannot make ourselves holier, but we can work with God as He creates a new sensitivity to growing into His image. Whimsy is an attitude of playful humor. I put whimsy and holiness together because I think combined they give us a great picture of someone who really cares about personal issues of integrity, moral growth, and pleasing God, as well as someone who can gently smile and keep a sense of humor around people who don't share our desires to please God. Religious people shoot for perfect holiness and call others to perfect holiness, and thus, judgment, comparison, and condemnation form a dense fog that blinds people from seeing God. A whimsically holy person can inspire people out of their mess without any judgment. They woo people through their intriguing character, and they charm people through their nonreligious ways. We see this holy whimsy when Jesus makes more wine for an already tipsy wedding party, when He sits down and enjoys laughter and a good meal with a corrupt

IRS agent named Levi, and when He rebukes His own disciples for getting mad at the children who wanted to get to Him. He was perfectly holy but never let His moral superiority keep people at a distance. Even though He never sinned, He was called a friend of sinners.

PRESENCE VERSUS PREOCCUPIED

There's a beautiful scene in Mark 5. A huge crowd had wedged Jesus into a corner, and people were smothering Him with their needs. A woman who had been struggling for years with a humiliating sickness somehow managed to make a desperate grab for His clothes. She made momentary contact and was healed. As she fell to the ground, overwhelmed with joy, Jesus turned around in the middle of the crowd and said, "Who touched my clothes?" (v. 30). Amazed at His awareness, the disciples answered, "You see the people crowding against you … and yet you can ask, 'Who touched me?'" (v. 31).

Today, people are used to everyone being preoccupied. With the flood of smartphones and constant email buzzes and sirens, short attention spans and lack of true attention are our way of life. That's why the attribute of presence is so otherworldly. When we sit down like Jesus did with a woman by a well and just chat, when we care enough to see people coming to us for help, or when we clear our schedules so that someone can come over and share an entire evening with us without any distractions, it is a game changer. If Jesus's own men were amazed at His awareness and presence, surely people around us will take notice as well.

EYES AND EARS VERSUS MOUTH

If you wanted to assemble a Mr. Potato Head so that he ended up looking as much like Jesus as possible, I'd suggest you put the big ears and eyes on him first. In fact, you should put the mouth on dead last. We see in Mark 10 a rich young man coming to Jesus for counsel. Listen closely to how this is worded: "Jesus looked at him and loved him" (v. 21).

Eyes are actually one of the most intimate parts of a person's body and reveal more than any other part. When you're feeling true empathy, those emotions create facial expressions that tell someone you really care about what he or she is saying or going through. Yet, when your eyes drop or close, or you look away or glance to the left or right, your expression screams, *I don't care. I've got other things on my mind.* Early in my ministry days, I took Cheryl to an intimate ordination exam. In front of eight men, Cheryl and I were grilled about our theological and Bible knowledge, our understanding of moral imperatives, our ministerial code of ethics, and a host of other "are you good enough?" questions. I distinctly remember one man rolling his eyes whenever Cheryl talked and another rotund man fighting like the dickens not to fall asleep. Eventually he succumbed, and we finished the ceremony with the man snoring like a trucker with a tube sock stuck in his throat. We left feeling dismissed, belittled, and bemused.

Eyes are a key part of incarnation. When they are open, the ears stay open, and when the ears listen, the heart softens—and soon the hands start moving to touch, help, and heal. But when the eyes are closed, the ears close, and the mouth opens. Words fly out, and quite frankly, the world doesn't want to hear any more of our religious rhetoric! Jesus looked at this young man and literally loved him. It wasn't just that He felt love for him. He was caring for this young man by the way He shut off His peripheral vision and gazed into his heart and soul. His eyes were an act of love.

RELATIONAL VERSUS TRANSACTIONAL

I was invited by a rather wealthy man to come to Canada to speak in his city. I was told that he was worth millions and that he had read my book and wanted some local pastors to hear me in person. He picked me up in his Bentley, and I enjoyed a great two days getting to know his story. On the way back to the airport, he said, "Hugh, I really appreciated getting to know you. I find it's rare to meet a man without guile." I thanked him, gave him a hug, and got on the plane. The first thing I did was open my computer and look up the word *guile*. Here's what it said: "Guile is a subtle deceptive nuance that compels a person to manipulate and distort relationships for personal gain." As I read, I was glad that this man thought I was free of this, but I felt incredibly convicted because I knew I wasn't! Throughout the two days, I was hoping that he might find my story and ministry interesting and write me a check for four bazillion dollars, and I stayed up later than I would have normally just so he would offer me a nip of his thirty-year-old scotch. I wasn't a man without guile! But I wanted to be.

In John 1:47, we read, "When Jesus saw Nathanael approaching, He said of him, 'Here is a true Israelite, in whom there is no guile'" (author's paraphrase). As Jesus was picking His disciples, He was impressed by this man. In the ancient Jewish culture, where deceit, fraud, and hypocrisy were the norm, Jesus lit up when He saw a man without wrong ambitions. He didn't say that Nathanael was without sin. But Jesus knew he was true and without trickery, and that as such, he would be a great addition to a team of men who would someday represent Jesus.

I think the reason this was so important to Jesus was that He wanted people to know that God is relational—truly relational without any impure or selfish motives. He wanted His Father to be trusted, and therefore He needed men and women who represented this. The psychology of agendas is that they make relationships transactional, which means that people are used for a purpose. People become a means to someone else's end, and this erodes a person's belief that he or she is valued regardless of any production.

Again, religious leaders have a real problem with this. Religion makes us want to build things and grow things and improve on things, and although none of those ambitions are bad in themselves, they cause a person to be expendable or valuable only if he or she plays along. Christians bent on converting a friend can do the same thing. We have to remember that how we treat people influences what they may believe about God, and if you look like you've got an agenda other than loving, listening, or blessing, your God will look like a conquistador instead of a compassionate King.

Most business relationships have to be transactional, as you are in fact trying to make a transaction, but in the realm of incarnational mission, it is high praise if someone says, "That person is without guile."

Jesus certainly had hopes for people, and He was faithful to His personal mission, but He didn't have an agenda. He had the highest calling of any man in the world, with only three years to complete the task and barely enough people to start a volleyball team. If anyone should have had their loincloth in a square knot, trying to assemble people for the dream team, whip them into shape, get 'em out there and get 'er done, it would have been Jesus. He should have been the most controlling, most intense, most transactional leader of all time, but He was the exact opposite and showed us how to never let goals take precedence over people.

CELEBRATION VERSUS SEGREGATION

This past weekend, I was driving my wife and daughter McKenna back from a wedding I performed in Winter Park, Colorado, for a young couple in our church. Watching my seventeen-year-old daughter looking out of the window with a content expression on her face, I asked, "McKenna, whatcha thinking about?" She smiled and said, "Nothing. I'm just really happy."

I didn't have to ask why. I knew why. We had just experienced two days of heaven. As we kept driving, two consecutive songs caught my attention and tied the whole weekend together. The first, by Coldplay, was called "'Til Kingdom Come," and just after that, Van Morrison sang the old classic "Into the Mystic."

Way back in the chapter "A New Gospel," we took some time to talk about the kingdom of heaven. Jesus, of course, tried to show us this mystical but tangible reality, and one of the pictures He used in the Gospels to capture our imagination of this newfound reality was that of a wedding ceremony.

The wedding we went to was held on Sunday, so I and about forty of our congregation missed the normal church gathering back down in Denver. Most of us got up there on Friday and had a day and a half to connect and meet people who had flown in from all over the country. Some of them shared our faith in Jesus, but most didn't. And it didn't matter. I suppose most folks tend to stick to their own cliques, but not our community. We all ate together, played together, shared stories, and mingled naturally with such robust love that surface conversations moved to depths you wouldn't think possible. As the hours and depth of celebration continued, you could feel a palpable friendship grow in everyone. Something mystical but tangible was occurring. People were experiencing the kingdom of God.

Our time there was filled with incredible food, fabulous wine, and bagpipes playing as we looked out over a winter wonderland. There were early morning coffee conversations and profound prayers and deep words of admiration and encouragement shared at the wedding rehearsal. We had late-evening nightcaps that deepened these new friendships. Broken families experienced healing, cars slid off icy roads, and acquaintances took care of one another. There was more great wine, dancing to live music, and on and on. If I could have frozen the moment in time, I would have. And that's the point. When you catch a waft of a real Jesus community, you want more. This was humanity as Jesus designed it. The kingdom of God was invisible but tangible.

Then the time for the wedding ceremony finally arrived. I, another pastor from our community, and a handful of others got to share our story of Jesus with a few hundred new friends. And it was received like an orphan receives a gift. There was no sense that we were pushing our faith on anyone. These new friends, of all levels of spiritual orientation or disorientation, smiled as we told the story they had been experiencing for two days.

Why was Jesus seen and talked about with such comfort? Simply this: God was seen in the context of human celebration, not human religiousness.

Next week, I'll head back to our Sunday church gathering. Everyone who was at the wedding will be there, and they will be doing the same thing. They will come in, enjoy food, and wait for others to arrive so they can laugh, hug, share more stories, and enjoy their crazy kids together, and it will take me at least thirty minutes to get them to move into the worship center. Oh … oops, I forgot to tell you. Celebration is worship! So we don't care if they move away from their conversations to come sit down and sing. Their song is their love for one another. But don't worry—the front rows are always full of Christians who come from other churches to "check us out." They usually bypass the party zone and quickly sit down with their Thomas Kinkade Bible covers and wait for "church" to begin.

I've learned over the years to just let them be. They get annoyed by how long it takes for us to start the formalities; they don't mix well in a community of the King that loves to celebrate, and they eventually leave. That's the way I like it.

EARTHY SAINTS

I hope this chapter has captured your heart. It's really the crux of this entire book. Our job description has nothing to do with starting or growing churches, converting friends, or changing the political landscape. Jesus modeled a life He wants us to live, and His hope for humanity is that you and I will learn to be truly human: earthy saints who reveal God's glory to anyone who happens to be watching or searching.

In John 17:22, Jesus said the same thing: "I have given them the glory that you gave me." That's amazing. God gave us His reflection! And even more, 2 Corinthians 3:18 sings, "And we who with unveiled faces all reflect the Lord's glory are being transformed into His likeness with ever-increasing glory" (author's paraphrase). And continuing the chorus is Colossians 1:27: "this mystery, which is Christ in you, the hope of glory." Consider this email I was thankful to receive.

Hey brother … Lindsey [Starbucks store manager] said she is going to start coming regularly to Adullam. She said she really liked that

   you admitted you weren't perfect

   you shared that you're a different guy today than you were twenty years ago

   you said the resurrection story is hard to believe

In short, it was your humanity that made all the difference for her. Just wanted to give you some encouragement and positive feedback. Proud of my pastor today.

                                    Jake

We matter in God's incarnational kingdom. We enjoy Him, we reflect Him, we bring glory to Him, and we become more like Him all the time! And in the end, it is Christ in us who is the hope of glory, the hope of the world! So go and be human and let God be God.

Think. What lightbulbs started to flicker during this chapter? What concepts were hard to reenvision? It will be the same for others, so if you're reading this book as a group, consider bringing your thoughts up the next time you gather.

Feel. What emotions do you feel when you picture Jesus saying, "Stop trying to be God; just be more human"?

Do. Go somewhere public this week and pray for people you see. Try not to protect yourself, but instead look at people deeply and ask God to show you His design for them.

6
OPENING ACT
Divine Setups

Have you ever had a brush with greatness and didn't know it? It's happened to me a few times. Most recently I was at a concert in Tuscaloosa, Alabama, as the incognito "spiritual adviser" of a band that was headlining. They gave me an all-access pass so I was able to walk wherever I wanted. I even got to raid the privately catered buffet that the famous people were using. To kill time, I went out to listen to the sound check of the opening act. I didn't know who she was, but I was mesmerized by her talent. Later, I headed back for round two at the buffet and asked one of the roadies, "So who's opening tonight?"

"Kelly Clarkson, sir," a young man replied. I thought her name sounded familiar, so I sent an email to my seventeen-year-old daughter and asked if she had ever heard of her. This was her reply: "Dad, you're a complete dork, and I hate you for being there without me."

Hmmm, whatever, I thought.

I headed to my friend's dressing room, where he and the boys were supposed to be getting ready. I was sort of taken aback to see they weren't there yet, but a pretty young girl was sitting on the couch. I introduced myself and asked, "So do you know the band?"

"Yes, I date Kevin."

We chatted for a while, and after I found out she had interests in acting, I naively asked, "So do you hope to make a living at this someday?"

Sheepishly she replied, "Yeah … I'm sort of working now … a little."

Because of the odd look on her face, I asked, "So … I have a strange question, but are you actually famous and I'm just too dorky to know about it?"

"Well, I don't know about the famous thing, but I'm on a show called *The Vampire Diaries*."

"Hmmm, that sounds familiar. Just for kicks, how about you and I take a picture, and I'll send it to my daughter." She was gracious, and I sent it off to McKenna just thirty minutes after the Clarkson incident.

My caption with the picture said, "Dad the dork just did it again. Do you know this gal?" In less than ten seconds came her reply: "I don't want to talk to you!!! Ahhhgggg!"

This experience taught me a great lesson about the way of incarnation: people don't recognize greatness until they are introduced to it, hear about it ahead of time, or see it for themselves. Humans are creatures of habit, and just like workers who head in to punch the clock every morning at the steel mill, people don't expect

or look for their lives to change. So when Jesus moves into the lives
of people, He begins a process of helping them receive Him.

JESUS HAD A FRONT BAND

Did you know that Jesus needed a couple of openers? For some reason, God knew that the Messiah couldn't just show up. Some buzz
and buildup were needed. People had to be prepared. God knew that
it is very difficult for people to believe in something that has never
shown up before. Remember, the Jewish people had been waiting for
a Messiah for about two thousand years. Their scripture was full of
references, promises, and innuendos, but generation after generation
came and went without realizing their hopes. To keep hope alive,
God sent prophets, but the last one came three hundred years before
Jesus, so things were pretty quiet on the streets.

If you've ever had a spiritual dry spell where it seems as though
God has stopped speaking to you, consider going twelve generations
without even a whisper. There were of course crazy impostor mes-
siahs who popped up here and there, but just as people stop looking
these days when a car alarm sounds, folks stopped looking up for the
real deal.

Like when a world-famous violinist plays in the subway, and no
one stops to recognize him or the greatness of his music, God must
have known ticket sales would go down unless He sent out a few
flares to pique some interest and get people ready for the real show.

The first two front bands were Mary and Zechariah. They both
prophesied that Jesus was the Messiah, and for a short time, they created some interest on the ground. There was also Simeon, a faithful

old Jewish man who patiently waited for the Messiah after an angel told him he would see Him before he died. He and a woman named Anna were there when Mary and Joseph presented Jesus, and they must have had their own little groundswell of curiosity and interest.

After Jesus was born, Mary and Joseph had to flee to Egypt. Eventually they came back and set up a home in Nazareth, but by then the hoopla had died down, and Jesus just grew up like any other Jewish kid.

THIRTY OF THE LONGEST YEARS OF YOUR LIFE!

As one of *those* dads, I make an absolute idiot out of myself when one of my daughters scores a goal in hockey, or sings the national anthem, or actually cleans up her room. I post Facebook notices, tweet, and tell all my friends if my girls do anything remarkable. If my boy was the Messiah, I'd probably make a little noise, but we have no indication that Joseph did anything but let Jesus grow up in a normal, quiet Jewish home. Maybe God told all of them to keep their cards tucked in, or maybe Mary and Joseph also, after a few years, began to doubt. Simeon and Anna both died off.

In Luke 3:23, we read an amazing scripture that most people miss. "Now Jesus himself was about thirty years old when he began his ministry." After getting almost no information about Jesus's upbringing, we watch Him emerge from what appears to have been a very quiet, normal Jewish life, without fanfare or even a karaoke performance. Can you wrap your mind around people waiting thousands of years for a hope, a Messiah? Someone to bring the world back into order? But God slowly played His pocket aces; He hid His sweepstakes card for three decades!

What was going on?

Preparation in many forms. And as we consider entering the lives of people, we must realize the subtle secrets of quiet seasons and of divine setups … and the power of letting God prepare our way into people's lives.

GOD IS AT WORK WHILE YOU'RE ASLEEP

Here's a big lightbulb moment about incarnational preparation: God has been at work way before anyone gets there—even before *you* get there.

Growing up in a Christian bubble, you can pick up some pretty lousy theology. One that stands out is this: people will perish if we don't get to them in time.

I suppose many of you reading that last sentence may still believe this, so let me ask you a question. How many people did you stop at work, the mall, or the street corner to speak to about Jesus today?

None? That's what I thought.

How about yesterday? Oh, none again? How about last year? Same answer? If that is the case, you may be liable for hundreds, if not thousands, of people missing out on heaven. Does that sound right? Does that feel right? Of course not. It is not right!

If you were God, would you leave the eternal fate of your precious sons and daughters in the hands of people only? Of course not, and even though we should feel compelled to be involved in the process, we must fight the urge to act presumptuously, move too fast, or think that the souls of the world hinge on our evangelistic attempts.

After a few thorough readings, I'm convinced that Scripture paints a picture of a God who pursues people over and over and is integrally a part of their stories from birth. It may not seem like it, but as you prepare others to know about Jesus, He is also preparing people to meet you. You are not responsible to close the deal, but you are a part of the deal. That makes you *important* in the process but not *responsible* for the process.

In Mark 4:26–29, Jesus was trying to teach about how things grow and emerge in His kingdom: "The kingdom of God is as if a man should scatter seed on the ground. He sleeps and rises night and day, and the seed sprouts and grows; he knows not how. The earth produces by itself, first the blade, then the ear, then the full grain in the ear. But when the grain is ripe, at once he puts in the sickle, because the harvest has come" (ESV).

We learn two important points. First, the man does get to scatter seed, and some of those seeds can be kind words or timely answers to what people are asking about, but they also include kingdom acts of service—silent prayers, a warm time over dinner, or a quick email encouraging someone's way. Second, and more important, is that all the growth is happening while the man is sleeping. This means he is not responsible to try to cause the growth or manipulate the end result. Paul said it another way in 1 Corinthians 3:6: "I planted the seed in your hearts, and Apollos watered it, but it was God who made it grow" (NLT).

The best words come from Jesus in John 5:16–17: "So the Jewish leaders began harassing Jesus for breaking the Sabbath rules. But Jesus replied, 'My Father is always working, and so am I'" (NLT). Jesus was saying that even on a day when men and women should be resting, God is still perusing around the minds, souls, and circumstances of people, so we can chill out and just sensitively saunter in when the coach calls.

But, "What if you are on an airplane and you have only one hour?" someone might ask. "Shouldn't you just dive right in and go for it?"

Again, if you believe people perish if you don't do what you perceive is "your job," then I guess you should. But if you believe God has been working in people's lives, pursuing them, trying to protect them from nut jobs who try to convert them every time they hop on a plane, then your job may be simply to be a Jesus follower who changes their assumptions. Maybe your role is to be kind, to provide an encouraging conversation, pick up the tab for their cheap airplane snacks, or offer help in getting their bags out of storage. These are all seeds of the kingdom.

FAILONI'S RESTAURANT ... LONGEVITY MATTERS

A year ago Cheryl and I were heading to Saint Louis to see our son. An old friend who had connections there said, "You've got to go to Failoni's Restaurant near where my family grew up." Failoni's is barely known to most people, but it's known to everyone who grew up in East Saint Louis. Alex Failoni, the owner, is there seven days a week and has been since he was a fetus. The night we showed up, he greeted us with free appetizers. He came over and shared stories with us, and I watched, intrigued, as he welcomed, hugged, and joked with every person by name. Failoni was a local legend, and I saw a bit of Jesus as I watched him pour drafts from the tap for all his friends. What was special about him? Just that he's been there on the same corner, every day, for a long time. If you want to see Alex sing some Sinatra songs, just google his restaurant.

As I'm writing this section, I'm sitting in a local haunt called Java on the Rock. It's a coffee hut right off the surf of Kona, Hawaii. I drove down from the hotel today and passed a little beach where about eight surfers were huddled under a tree. Their bronzed, leathered skin was tatted with ancient tribal symbols; their hair was either gone or graying, showing their deep age well into their sixties. Like ancient ruins, they just sat there like guardians of the surf. I found out that the beach was sacred and that many a "haole" has found this out when trying to surf there without permission. My buddy Matt, who lives near there, says that if you walk past them to head out and hang ten, you may not even make it to the beach. These men have put in their time, and you'd be wise to ask their permission and get their blessing.

There's something really powerful about meeting native-born locals who have been in the same spot their entire lives. They have unique stories and a street-level understanding of minute cultural distinctives, and they can tell you just by watching the skies and smelling the trade winds how the day is going to go.

Jesus was a native, and He lived most of His life in the same neighborhood. If you would have come in as a stranger, Jesus would have taken you around to any business, bar, or hotel and would have been able to introduce you by name to everyone in town. He would have known what the weather was going to be like, what fruits were in season, where to get the best handmade crafts and clothing, and where to find the best spot to watch the sunset.

Jesus's town of Nazareth was known as "the hood." As He started to emerge from His thirty years of underground life, people would say things like, "Can anything good come out of Nazareth?" (John 1:46 ESV). It was known as a community "you might want to avoid." The people were crude and rude, and the land not as productive as other places. It was like saying you were from South Chicago, Detroit, or Vegas. Everyone had jokes about this place and its people, but Nazareth was the place Jesus called home.

Longevity is a hidden secret for those who truly want incarnational fruit. If Jesus spent thirty years becoming known, building a reputation, becoming a man of the people, maybe we should reconsider the transient nature of our lives.

I live in Denver, Colorado. People here change their housing locations every eighteen months on average. That includes those who live in the suburbs. As our economy has struggled, as families have been blown apart, as people try to navigate normal life, the new norm is to move around. I tell pastors to mentally prepare to view the ministry in their church just like they would view a college ministry. Expect to have only two to four years with people.

Though everyone's on the go, we can make intentional decisions not to be.

Incarnation has a home, and over the course of our lives, we'll probably have the most impact if we can stay put in an area and be the one constant in a constantly shifting world. I realize that the future economy looks bleak and that you will feel pressure to move whenever you can upgrade, but Jesus honors our prayers and plans to stick around. Incarnational fruit doesn't just happen. It happens over time, and the more time we can give to a community, a street, a school, a sports club, or a pub, the more impact we will have.

LET OTHERS SPEAK ABOUT YOU

If being a hometown boy or girl is part of your persona, eventually someone's going to talk to others about you. For Jesus it happened when His cousin John was out in the wilderness, drawing attention to Him. John was baptizing people with a general call to repentance, and one day as Jesus walked toward him and his followers, John pointed at Jesus and said, "Behold, the Lamb of God, who takes away the sin of the world!" (John 1:29 ESV). Some who had become deeply drawn to John wondered what to do, and John quickly diverted his own followers to Jesus, saying, "I'm not worthy to untie that guy's sandals" (v. 27, author's paraphrase). And "I must become less so that He can become more" (3:30, author's paraphrase).

Here is a truism. What you say about yourself matters very little, but what others say of you means the world.

I once offered up a free paint job during a church auction to raise money for a cause. I figured an elderly woman would bid a thousand dollars on a quick two- to three-day job and I could help someone in need without it costing too much. Sadly, fifty bucks got my services. I drove out one morning to meet my client, and as I headed into a very rich neighborhood called the Northwest Hills of Portland, I realized that I might be in a pickle. All the homes were huge, and many of them were positioned on cliffs overlooking downtown. I prayed, but my worst fears were realized. The house was huge, and the back of the home was four stories high on stilts, overhanging a cliff full of blackberry briars.

In that moment I decided to feign illness. But as I put my head on the steering wheel to collect myself, a very gentle but very strong message entered my mind: *Paint the house.*

I knew it was God, but I sat there another thirty minutes to make sure.

Eventually, with drooping head and shoulders, I knocked on the door. Out came Ralph, and we talked over the job. The last words I remember him saying were, "Oh, and I'd like you to hand paint it with a brush instead of using your paint sprayer so we don't get any overspray on the plants." *Perfect*, I thought. *I should be done just about the time Jesus returns to earth.*

For the next four weeks, Ralph and I became friends. Sort of like Sylvester and Tweety Bird.

I tell you this story because at the time, I couldn't find God in any of this. I actually thought that I was wasting precious finances and ministry time. It made no sense at all. Until I met Ralph's son.

Scott, a local businessman, found out that I had stuck it out with his crazy dad and was so impressed he eventually joined our church and became my greatest personal friend and financial advocate. He helped fund our church plant, and he also bought me a condo that we sold later so we could acquire an awesome mountain getaway spot for my family.

In 1 Thessalonians, Paul gushed about a small church by saying that word about them had echoed and reverberated through the countryside (1:8). People always talk, and if we live with their voices in view, it will calm us down and help us lock into the neighborhood. We are the opening acts for one another—and for Jesus—and we play a huge role in preparing people for their future faith. Don't think the whole process is up to you, but you really do matter! The more your street cred rises, the easier it will be for your friends to point to you and for you to point people to Jesus.

AN APPOINTED TIME

I know what some of you are saying to yourselves. "Hugh, please don't give me that same old line that Saint Francis did about sharing the gospel at all times and if necessary using words! Do we ever get to speak about Jesus?" Yes, we do, and we will spend a few chapters on it later, but there is what Jesus called an "appointed time."

It is crazy to watch Jesus work the clock. Often He would heal someone and then say, "Don't go tell anyone." One time He strongly urged a man to stay quiet after He healed him. I'm not sure what "strongly urge" looks like in your mind, but I picture Jesus trying to calm down this poor man who couldn't contain his excitement and thankfulness, grabbing him by the scruff of his shirt, pulling his spitting, sputtering face within an inch of His own, and saying, "Listen, knucklehead; I know you're fired up about this right now, but seriously, don't go blabbing about this. I'm not kidding!"

Why wouldn't Jesus just want everyone to start touting His powers? Why wouldn't He want to go on a healing tour? No one knows for sure, but Jesus knew how circumstances link together in a chain of responses, and He was a master at doing only what He saw His

Father doing. Timing of when truth comes out is as important as the truth itself.

There is an appointed time for you to speak as well. Moments happen when God is clearly leading you to speak up about Him, ask a great question, or perhaps grab someone by the hand and say, "I really want to bring up something that has been on my heart about you." Living a life to bring glory to God and helping others perceive God's glory involves

> the art of living well (not perfectly)
> praying for insight and wisdom
> responding to the sensitive nuances of each person
>> you're trying to love the way Jesus would love

In other words, learning the art of incarnational living will help you learn the art of incarnational speaking.

In John 17, as Jesus was praying to the Father about His three years of formal ministry, He said this: "I have ... finish[ed] the work you gave me to do" (v. 4).

A couple of questions are in order. Had Jesus healed everyone at this point? No. Had Jesus taught everyone, fed everyone, and helped everyone? Of course not. Had He prepared the disciples to know exactly what to do upon His departure? Not even close. Yet Jesus knew that He had finished what God asked Him to do.

Here is what goes through my head:

- I rarely feel like I'm doing enough.
- I almost always feel that I could do more.

- I'm failing in the opportunities that God brings
  my way.
- I tend toward cynicism and apathy because I
  don't think my little efforts will do much for the
  kingdom anyway.

But the more I study Jesus and see Him letting God dictate who, when, how, how long, how much, and how often, I find some peace in knowing that God has always showed up before me, that He will be there after I'm gone, and that He loves these people infinitely more than I and will continue to pursue them after my life has rubbed up against theirs.

That blows my feelings of inadequacy out of the water. Most of the time, I'm able to look at everyone as a friend and every fleshy moment as an opportunity to help move someone just a few inches closer to seeing God's glory. Stop for just a second now, and think about the totality of your life and the influence God wants to give you with the people He loves. Your life can be like a thirty-year slow dance, a thirty-year scotch, or a thirty-year oak tree that grows up and gives shade to many. God knows the appointed times for you, too. He knows when it will be time to let you lead, when to uncork you, and when you are ready to cover others. But don't miss the beauty of Jesus's life. He had thirty years of submerged incarnation before His three years of emerged ministry.

Think. What circumstances in your life might God be using right now to cause people to speak well of you?

Feel. Have you ever thought about picking a city or community to stay put in? What does this level of commitment cause you to feel? Afraid? Excited? Something else?

Do. This week, consider picking two local spots as your go-to joints. These spots could be a coffee shop, pub, fitness center, or restaurant. Make it your goal to get to know every employee by name. Start acting like a native.

7

WORKERS' COMP

Redeeming the Curse of Labor

It was my junior year of college, and I was broke. Realizing that next semester's $3,500 bill was looming, I went down to a local paint store and asked the manager how a youngster like myself could learn how to paint houses for a living. He gave me about thirty minutes of his time and soon filled my Honda hatchback full of brand-new gear. I spent that day and the next nailing signs on telephone poles around Seattle to try to get work.

Within two hours I got my first call, and by the end of the summer I had put away $10,000 for the next school year.

At the time, I was so thankful that I would be able to finish my college degree, but I had no idea how important this trade would be to God's call on my life.

I'm now forty-six and haven't had to paint a house for four years. With a bad back, I'm quite content to make a part-time living from speaking and training other leaders around the globe, but I will never lament the twenty-some years God blessed me with a trade that would sustain my full-time calling to ministry.

Wait. Read that last statement again. I want to make sure you caught this incarnational key: my worldly vocation was directly connected with my calling as a vocational minister. I received my call to ministry from God when I was a sophomore in college, and I remember it like it was … today. I woke up and knew that every waking moment would now be about helping the lost, leery, and least find faith in Jesus. I just knew it! I changed my major to religion and psychology and upon graduation went right into seminary. From there it was ten years with Youth for Christ, then I made the transition into our first church plant. And although each phase of full-time ministry changed drastically, one common gift held it all together. My job as a painter. I unknowingly experienced the power of seeing my secular life as inextricably linked to my sacred calling.

As my family grew, expenses grew and the stakes got higher, but I never varied from my morning and evening prayers that went something like this: "Lord, thanks for how You always provide, so send me work or send me money. I'll respond to whatever way You choose to bless me."

And it worked.

When He sent money from supporters of our ministry, I would fill my days with people, nonstop. And when He sent me work, I would increase my intentionality of meeting with people for early morning breakfasts, lunches, and late-night gatherings in our home or a local pub. It wasn't easy, and I always preferred option A, but learning to balance the sacred and secular was, and still is, the most empowering skill to living as an incarnational missionary.

CALLED TO WHAT?

As I write this, I'm sitting in the Denver ChopHouse in terminal A. Two young guys in their midtwenties are sitting right behind me, talking about finishing seminary. One is deciding between staying in seminary forever as a theology professor or taking a church job. The other guy wants to move right into a senior-pastor position. Excuse me while I pull away from you for a moment and try an experiment to see if I can get these guys to consider working a job. I'll be right back.

Twenty minutes later …

Okay, so I just met Josh and Evan. Both are newly married, and Josh has a two-year-old son. I bought their dinner, so they were happy to chat, but the talk didn't go so well. I let them know that in ten years America will be as unchurched as the United Kingdom, Europe, Canada, Australia, Portland, or Boulder and that there probably won't be many churches looking for pastors. And even if they choose to start a new church, they won't be able to make a full-time living for quite a while because people don't give as much to churches anymore. Also, seminaries, denominations, and other structures that have been formally tied to the growth of local churches and their financial support will also begin to tighten up on spending as they struggle to survive.

I asked them the big question I ask most young wannabe ministers: "If there were no churches to pay you to be professional Christians, what would you do to provide for your wife and kids while you answer the full-time call to ministry?"

Evan was open to my question and said that he was presently working for UPS and could conceive of doing that for a while but couldn't wait to get out of it so he could serve God fully in a church. Josh said, "Well, if I had to work a real job, then I wouldn't feel that I had a full-time call to ministry at all. I'd feel like I would have to pick one or the other." He continued, "I also don't think God would ask someone to be so focused on ministry to people and still have to hassle with the normal pressures and fatigue that come with a normal job."

After listening for a while, I said, "Guys, did you know that from the time Jesus was old enough to work, He did? As a Jewish boy, and then a Jewish man, Jesus put in a nine-to-five until He was thirty." They looked at me like the thought had never occurred to them before. Then I mentioned the apostle Paul's bivocational life after his conversion, as well as that of the disciples, and reminded them of many great saints throughout history who had massive influences on the movement while sustaining their own livelihood. John the Baptist, Barnabas, Priscilla and Aquila, Saint Patrick, John Wesley, and John Calvin, just to name a few.

"Guys, the gospel got to you and me primarily through men and women who were lawyers and plumbers, prostitutes, meat carvers, or folks who just lived off their own land. And the day is coming fast when the gospel will again pass through the lives and ministries of normal people who have a full calling to ministry but also have a trade."

Of course, many great spiritual leaders were also supported by churches, or even the government, and there's nothing inherently wrong with making a living from the work of the gospel. But every Jesus follower is called to full-time service to Jesus. Our movement as a whole has been hurt by the notion that only a small percentage of humans are called to ministry.

So what is up with this idea of *calling*? The word actually means to be "set apart." In the Old Testament, God set apart the family or line of Aaron as a priestly line. People born to this tribe grew up knowing that they would follow their grandfathers, fathers, and brothers into a more dedicated branch of the Jewish people, and as such, they would tend to the religious customs, needs, and traditions related to the temple, to the scriptures, and to the daily guidance of the Jewish people. These designated people continued until the time of Jesus, but there were also several other groups of people who seemed a bit more "set apart." The Pharisees or teachers of the law were a distinct group that lived a more religiously legalistic life. They were the holders of truth and knowledge, and they gave the marching orders to the Jewish religious affairs (often corrupted by political and financial power that kept everyone toeing the line). The Sadducees were an upper-class spiritual sect that hung around and kept watch over the temple.

Neither of these groups was Jesus's favorite.

There were also the Essenes (ancient-day monastics), who lived away from the city and focused on simplicity and perfect holiness. Intermixed with all of these groups were countless rabbis teaching their own small bands of followers. In every case, these people felt "set apart"; their lives were uniquely called of God, unlike the normal townspeople.

What made the life of Jesus so peculiar was that when He came, He called a band of men and women who fit none of these categories. They were what you might call "peasants." The disciples were of mundane stock. Some fishermen, a doctor, some carpenters, tax collectors, and the rest just standard dudes. The women who assembled around Jesus and His mission were most likely working the land or had simple jobs selling their wares. One notable woman had actually made her living from selling her body. Clearly her trade must have shifted as she joined Jesus's inner circle, but she, along with every other disciple, supported the mission through a trade. Then after the disciples, we see men like Paul become *apostles*—the new name for the new leaders of Jesus's movement. Paul, who was a part of the very powerful sect of Pharisees prior to his conversion, had to leave his "set apart" vocation with the upper-crust spiritual elite and work his apostleship as a normal man with a day job. In other words, as Jesus exalted Paul in true spiritual influence, He had to first get him out of the spiritual-political bubble he was in.

Consider these words about our calling:

> You are called to pray at all times (1 Thess. 5:17),
>> work with your hands, and live a simple life (4:11).
> If you will not work, you shall not eat (2 Thess. 3:10).
> You are all called as priests unto our God (1 Pet. 2:9).
> You all have been given the ministry of reconcilia-
>> tion (2 Cor. 5:18–19).

For those who are interested, we will spend a little more time on the pro-pastor thing in a minute, but I don't want you to miss the hand that is waving right in front of our faces. These verses are for every man and woman.

God's kingdom needs laborers of all kinds.

Jesus even taught His disciples to pray that the Lord of the harvest would send out more laborers into the field. Interestingly, He didn't specifically say more leaders, or more vocational ministers, or more priests, or paid bishops. Just the word *laborers*. In Lance Ford's book *UnLeader* he wrote,

> Depending on the translation, at the very most, "leader" is used only six times in the New Testament, while the word "servant" can be found over two hundred times. We should be asking why those of us who have a calling to serve the church obsess so much more over leadership than servant-ship. Jesus said, "I am among you as the one who serves" (Luke 22:27). If we honestly want to be like Jesus—if we honestly want to follow Jesus—we will pursue servantship rather than leadership. We will work to become the greatest servants we can be.[1]

I'm a firm believer in true leadership as influencing people toward God's end, but even what we call leadership gifts as mentioned in Ephesians 4 (apostles, prophets, evangelists, shepherds, teachers) are entirely servant gifts that build up the rest of God's family. The saints (better understood as peasant workers) are the ones called to do the works of ministry. This means the paid pros are supposed to equip normal people to do most of the heavy lifting in God's kingdom. Yet today, many vocational ministers are stuck doing the work of minis-try because they take a paycheck from consumer Christians who fail to see the full scope of their calling.

All are called as ministers and priests unto God. All are called to work and provide for basic needs (if we can), and everyone's lot in life has the same sacred/secular potential as God's hand directs and uses it all. Jesus worked and Paul worked, and if you get stuck in the blessed curse of hard labor—be it the bank, brewery, or bookstore—there's an uncommon joy in learning to redeem the curse for God's glory.

JESUS STUCK WITH THE CURSE

I'm in an accountability group with four men here in Denver. Each man has a very unique calling around the world and in our city, but one fella named Dave is a real work of art. Dave's vision for helping churches come together in Denver captured the imagination of a law firm owner. This man offered Dave a full salary to work a few hours a week blessing some of his clients, and Dave gets to use the rest of his time for ministry purposes. While riding down a fairway one day, Dave said, "Hugh, I have an amazing life. I get a full-time salary to take clients out golfing, to Bronco games, or really nice dinners. And then I get all my extra time to try to change the city of Denver. Hugh, I have escaped the *curse!*"

I have to admit, I was jealous, so as I approached a 215-yard 3-iron, I looked up from my practice swing and said, "Dave, the more I think about it, the more I realize you must be God's favorite. Even Jesus didn't escape the curse!"

In Genesis, right after Adam and Eve allowed sin to make its home on terra firma, God told Adam that as part of the natural consequence of sin, he and the rest of us humans would now have to labor in the dirt. Simply put, we would have to toil and work a job. We all know we deserve (and need) this, but have you ever actually pondered the fact that Jesus, in coming to earth, also humbled Himself and submitted to our curse of work?

I can imagine the conversation between the Father and Jesus about what incarnating His life would entail. They must have talked about temptation, women, betrayal, how to handle all the politics, how to develop servant-leaders, and of course what death on the cross would be like. Those would have been sobering thoughts, even as the Father and Son were firmly focused on eternity. But it must have been a strange moment when Jesus realized that He not only was going to die for the curse but also would have to work by the curse for many years! One thing is for sure—Jesus likely had some bad days at work like the rest of us.

Can you think of your worst day at work? I can.

It was a hot August day. I was painting a brand-new sixteen-unit condo complex. I was on the roof, trimming out all the gutters and fascia boards. Because of the amount, I had taken a five-gallon jug of white paint up on the asphalt roof. I propped the paint can with two-by-fours so the can would be solidly even and stable. I placed tarps underneath so I wouldn't get any drips on the roof. I soon began taking trips to fill my smaller can as I moved along the complex. I did everything right.

And then, amid everything right, everything went wrong. To this day I have no explanation except that a huge pterodactyl from hell must have been sent by Lucifer to knock over the can. I heard a smack, then a whoosh, and then I turned around to watch five gallons of latex pour over the roof and down onto the brand-new driveway. I was stunned. "For crying out loud! For the sake of Pete! For the love of God and all that's merciful!"

Actually, I *wish* those were the words I said.

I tried to start wiping it up but then stepped in the paint—and in my frantic frenzy made it look like the Detroit Lions football team had walked all over the roof! *Ahh!* I got to the ground but remembered there was no water on the job site because of it being new construction. So reverting back to my days as a delinquent, I quickly climbed a twelve-foot cyclone fence, went unit by unit "borrowing" everyone's hoses, strung together about eight lengths, turned on the water, and then spent eight hours wire brushing the paint off the roof. *Argh!!!!*

It didn't work!

I had to cover the cost of a new roof and spent six weeks essentially painting for free. I'll tell you what—I've never had more vibrant conversations with God as I did that summer. My attitude was pushed to the breaking point, my bank account went dry, and my theology was, well … a little shaken. I was in the middle of my first year at a new church, and I was absolutely befuddled that God didn't seem to care about all the wasted time and money from this one day of painter hades.

As was my rhythm, I met with a group of men every Tuesday for a "Jesus time," and even though I was trying to be the leader, I finally told them what happened. After I shared the story, I said, "So I hope you guys are okay with having a pastor who is actually an atheist!" The boys rallied, put their arms around me, and became the men of God I needed in that hour of trial. I noticed over the rest of the summer that my stock rose significantly with these men—all because they knew I went through the ups and downs of real life like they did.

When I realize that Jesus had days like this but never pulled the God card and took a pass at tribulation, I respect His incarnation more and more. I see His redeeming purpose. His job gave Him street cred. His job gave Him relational connection with the commoners. His job gave Him an opportunity to show people a different attitude and a different work ethic and displayed the glory of His character. His job was not just a cover. His job was part of the redemption process. He was breaking the curse and showing us how to do the same.

THE BLESSINGS OF THE CURSE ... RETURN OF THE TRAPPISTS!

Okay, so let's stop talking misery and get into the fun stuff. We can learn a lot about the sacred and secular from some of our earliest brothers and sisters. My favorites were called Trappist monks. They followed the Rule of Saint Benedict: *Ora et labora*, which was Latin for "Pray and work." There were, of course, other monastic orders, and many struggled to survive, but the Trappists were known for being self-sufficient communities. Unlike some monastic communities that lived far away from the local city center, Trappists often lived out their cloistered lives in close proximity to town so that their products would be a blessing to people and so that they could sustain their own calling to pray and work. They baked bread, crafted beer, raised livestock, and hosted guests like any modern-day resort. Apparently about 20 to 30 percent of the entire economic output in medieval times came from their agricultural and creative enterprises. Amazingly, at the time of the Reformation, a third of all the land in England was owned by these sacred secularists! Rodney Stark, in his book *The Victory of Reason: How Christianity Led to Freedom, Capitalism, and Western Success*, said that capitalism was invented in monasteries in the ninth, tenth, and eleventh centuries. The reason was that these men, unlike the greedy, self-oriented society, actually believed that God was letting them steward His resources and followed the call to bless people and create sustainable products in line with God's heart for them. They dealt with integrity, compassion, creativity, and hard work, and it changed the world.

Again, not all monastic orders place such a high value on business enterprise. The Franciscans and Dominicans, like Buddhist monks, have to depend on charity and donations and sometimes stand on street corners, begging for help. They believe that, like Jesus, those who are "set apart" will be provided for. Again, I don't think it's helpful to dissuade people from being dependent on others, but as you consider your own calling, I want you to be aware that there are options. Missiology requires that we ask, "Based on the world as it exists today, with the unique economic, social, and global issues facing people, what is my best response and option for blessing people and sustaining my life?" I believe that in most centuries, as in the time we live in today, those who take the Trappist approach may enjoy life and do more good than those who wait on others to empower their passion.

MODERN-DAY TRAPPISTS

Quite a few people got to know me through the first book I wrote, *The Tangible Kingdom: Creating Incarnational Community*. It was a simple story of how a handful of friends moved to Denver to try to make God's kingdom tangible. Everyone in our little community worked a normal job, but we made sure to create some intentional rhythms of life around Jesus's teaching about the kingdom. We figured that if we made the kingdom tangible and lived a good-news life, others might just naturally be drawn to us and our God. Well, it worked. We didn't have a church to go to for almost three years, so we just worked our jobs and then committed many of our meals, our free weekends, and any spare moment to community, communion, and blessing. Everyone belonged, everyone got blessed, and we enjoyed seeing our secular lives reveal the sacred things God was up to.

Today, Adullam is nearly ten years old. We are substantially larger and have enough money to pay several full-time pastors, but we have chosen to maintain our bivocational model. We have no full-time staff. As I said before, I don't feel that there is anything bad about having a full-time pastor, but our little portion of the body of Christ is making the intentional choice to work in the world, simply because it seems to give us more street cred, more natural interaction with the culture, and less need to put money into prop-ping up a program to keep consumer Christians content. Although it is often more difficult to manage life, our struggle is everyone's to share, and it helps the Christians who join our community know that their lives, vocations, and struggles matter deeply. Every penny and every second we give to others *counts*. We are a community of full-time missionaries all serving undercover as moms, dads, teach-ers, engineers, coaches, contractors, and baristas. If you want more information on how to live what we call a BiVO life (bivocational), we wrote an entire book on the subject called *BiVO*.

I am the senior leader, though I still work thirty hours a week in the world. It's tough, but I love the freedom and opportunity and inspiration it gives our whole team and congregation. Because we've made this choice collectively, our monthly budget to hold our church together is about one-sixth of what the normal American church costs. We therefore get to shift most of our resources of time, talent, and treasures back to where God intended them to be. Back into the lives of those we are on mission for.

We believe wholeheartedly in and structure our community around what is called the *tsaddiqim*. This is a Hebrew word that means "the righteous." Specifically the reference is to people who follow God and bring blessing or shalom to a city. In Proverbs 11:10 we read, "When the righteous prosper, the city rejoices." As Jesus brings the reality of a new kingdom into the kingdom of darkness in this world, God's people stand out because as they prosper, the whole city prospers. There's no individualized evangelical faith within the tsaddiqim, but rather a community of Jesus followers who place the foci of their personal faith squarely on the idea of being stewards of God's kingdom resources together for the shalom or peace of the people around them.

This whole idea is wrapped up in a word we've lost the meaning for. The word is *blessing*. In the church leadership world, we always talk about being "missional," which means to be sent. To make the idea stick, I often ask, "Sent to be and do what?" And the answer is that every Jesus follower is sent to be a blessing. Blessing means to make God's favor or His ways tangible to people. Therefore, in the incarnational life, each of us measures the goal, the process, and the ultimate progress by how much tangible blessing we bring to people.

And the most well-known blessing is found in the Jewish concept called *shalom*.

Shalom is another way of saying, "God's original design." There are four primary spheres of redemption that we get to bring to the world.

1. Peace with God
2. Peace with self
3. Peace with others
4. Peace with creation

Shalom is not a blessing you pray over people. Shalom is a reality you get to bring over souls through beauty; friendship; physical health; crisis intervention and recovery; security; and lack of violence, injustice, abuse, and hunger. Shalom allows us to bring economic security, education, and the dignity of vocation to those without work.

Because the tsaddiqim are in every nook and cranny of society, every job we have is a "green" job. We, as Scripture says, "do [everything] … as to the Lord" (Col. 3:23 NKJV), revealing God's good news through the integrity by which we work, by making every workplace safer, more joyful, more transformative, and more profitable. Today, as I pen these words, the greatest need we have in our own faith community is for someone to help people find jobs. If you can grow a business and see it as your mission, you will be huge in kingdom influence.

As God's righteous people band together to leverage all their gifts, passions, and resources, we will naturally link together with

God's heart for the neighborhoods and cities we live in. That eventually makes us become relevant to the felt needs of people. God's design of redeeming the workplace is front and center in His plan to redeem the world. You just have to let God bring blessing to what right now feels like a curse. It's time to stop grumbling about your job and begin looking for shalom to bust through your mundane and turn it into a miracle for someone else.

BACK TO THE SEMINARY BOYS

You may be wondering about all of us "professional saints." Is it possible that those two seminary men could find jobs and have blessed lives serving within a church? Absolutely. In Scripture there are three primary forms of financial funding. And all are fine. You just have to pick the one that best suits you. The first is that of a fully paid saint. Be it a pastor, a missionary, or a priest, a workman is worthy of his hire (1 Tim. 5:18). If you take a job that is primarily designed to free you up to serve the needs of an existing congregation, that is fine and good. Get on with it, but make sure you are equipping God's people instead of doing the work for them.

Plan B is more like the bivocational post I am living or that Paul lived. Sometimes Paul would try to raise money so that another guy could be freed up for Plan A, but for himself, he decided to work among the people so as not to be a burden (1 Thess. 2:9; 2 Thess. 3:8). This was Paul the missionary understanding that he would have more influence if he had at least a part-time job. The third option is that of being fully occupational, working any job you can find that gives you a chance to be righteous and bring shalom to others. What's great is that all are equally rich with calling. All are equally holy, and God blesses all.

PICK YOUR PAIN

I should also mention that all three options are hard. The corporate path is just as brutal as the congregational path. The curse is still the curse, and making a full-time income from ministry ain't any easier. Work is work! I've been pastoring now for twenty-five years, and very rarely do people call because they are having an awesome day. The life of a pastor is one of being on call for all the wrong stuff. The pay for most of us small-church guys isn't nearly what it's cracked up to be, and although pastors may seem to avoid some of the mess of real work, they actually live with the sum total of the mess of an entire congregation. That means nearly every day they drive home focusing on something bad. The job is never done, their motives are always in question, and they are actually the least positioned to make a difference in a normal person's life for simply that reason. They don't live a normal life. So cut them some slack. They are taking one for the team!

So in the end, ask God which option fits you best and see what doors open up. Don't overspiritualize your "ministry" job, and don't underspiritualize your mundane job. Give God room to bring the sacred out of the secular, and He will.

Think. Try to think of the chain of people who brought the gospel message and life to you. How many of them were normal people with normal jobs? What does that tell us about God's plan to reach the world?

Feel. How often do you lament your job under your breath or to someone else? Our mundane jobs don't feel very good, and our vocations are full of hard moments that weigh heavily on our hearts. This is the curse! Consider how you might feel if you looked for ways to redeem the curse and bring glory to God in your attitude, how hard you work, and who you encourage each day.

Do. Consider writing down a prayer of declaration to God about the job you have—what you will commit to always do, what you will never do, and how you'd like to use this job to bring shalom to others. Post this short mission statement in your workspace.

8

TURNING TABLES

Pick Some Fights for God

It was about five degrees out, and I had just pulled into a gas station to fill up my truck. I jumped out quickly, stuck my card in the self-pay slot, and found myself muttering as the computer kept delaying my gas purchase with silly questions.

"Do you want to use debit or credit?" *I'll pay in drachmas if you'll speed it up, sparky!*

"Do you want a car wash?" *No—my windshield would crack!*

"Do you want a receipt?" *Yeah, and I'll use the paper as insulation in my underwear!*

The gas robot finally let me begin pumping, so as soon as the ticker started, I jumped back into my car to warm up. As I sat there, staring out the front window, my eye caught a man sitting down on the street corner, holding a sign up asking for help. As you know, these nameless individuals are ubiquitous, and it's easy to forget they are real people.

But not this time.

I barely got gas in the tank without passing out from hypothermia, so how could this guy be surviving? I was overcome with curiosity as much as concern for this man. I reached down into my side door console and pulled out two handfuls of spare coins, put on my hat, zipped up my coat, and made my way to the corner.

Expecting the man to be mentally ill, I was blown away when he looked up and said, "How's your morning going, sir?" Because of the beautiful inflection of his voice and his kind tone, I knelt down right in front of him, hoping to shield his face from the arctic wind.

"I'm doing well today, but how are you making it through this cold?" I asked.

Without a tone of manipulation, he responded, "Yeah, it's a pretty tough day today, but I'm thankful; I've been out here when it was much colder."

Amazed by his humanness, I told him I had a few coins for him. As he tried to cup his frozen hands, copper and silver began to fall through the cracks in his fingers. He made intense eye contact with me and stammered out, "Sir, I really appreciate the help today, but my hands are too cold to grab these coins. Is there any way you could take them back and see if the gas-station attendant can turn them into dollars or, better yet, just buy me a coffee?"

At that moment, I was incredibly grieved at myself. It was like the anger of God came over me about … me! My self-talk sounded like, *Halter, you dipwad. Instead of cleaning out your spare change, why didn't you just give him a ten-dollar bill!*

"What's your name, sir?" I asked. He told me, and as I gently scraped the coins back out of his hands, picked up the ones that had fallen onto the pavement, I said, "Joe, hold on just a minute. I'm going to run in and grab you a few things." I left Joe in the frigid air and went into the minimart, where I filled up a bag with food and got hot coffee and some toiletries before running back out. On the way, I stopped and grabbed a blanket I had in my truck, an extra pair of shoes, and some spare gloves. I knelt back down by Joe, folded up the blanket as a mat, and spread it out next to where he was sitting. "Joe, can I help you sit down on this blanket? I think it will be warmer for you." I picked him up, gently set him on the blanket, put the gloves on his frozen, statue-like hands, got his coffee for him, and stuck a twenty-dollar bill in his pocket. Joe just looked at me and winked.

Returning to my warm truck, I slowly drove off. I had a hard time seeing the road as my eyes started to fill up. I was so disappointed by my blindness. I was so mad at my insensitivity. I was so sad that Joe would sit there all day and freeze, and then I was overcome with even deeper emotion that my small moment of goodness was such a fight. I've never been that angry with myself.

Incarnational living isn't just about being nonjudgmental, nonreligious, or superloving. Fleshy faith isn't just about grabbing a beer with neighbors, having friends who are gay, or mowing your neighbor's yard. Incarnation is ultimately about representing and revealing the real God to people. And the real God sometimes gets really ticked about what happens in His world. He is a God of love. But He is just as much a God of justice, so if you're going to follow Him and be like Him, you're occasionally going to need to pick a fight or fight for things He cares about. If you don't, He may pick a fight with you.

RAGE

John 2 is my favorite chapter in the Bible. It begins with the first miracle Jesus ever did, turning water into wine at a wedding party. I could wax on about the incarnational beauty of Jesus being the "party guy," but what happened just after this is what really captures my intrigue. The next morning, while the rest of the party was recovering, Jesus took His mother, His brothers, and His disciples into Capernaum for a few days and then walked to Jerusalem for the Passover. In one of the most surprising scenes recorded in Scripture, Jesus became enraged as He watched people selling religious items, exploiting the poor, and using the temple and religion as a means to make money.

You might think Jesus simply "lost it" and went postal, but as verse 15 indicates, He pulled away quietly, found some supplies, and intentionally made a whip out of leather cords. Like Clint Eastwood, Jesus deliberately but thoughtfully entered a hostile saloon, came back to where all the action was, and scattered the crowd. Chaos erupted! The sound of Jesus's whip whistling through the air, reverberating off the stone walls, captured everyone's attention and respect. As the cows and sheep went running, salesmen who wanted to attack Jesus couldn't because they had to chase down their animals. But Jesus wasn't finished! He went over to where the money changers were, and as they frantically tried to keep people in line, He grabbed the underside of the rough wood tables, knocking them over like a house of cards. Pigeons went flying overhead, people screamed, and you could still likely hear Jesus yelling something along the lines of "Get rid of all this crap … don't jack with My Father's house … this ain't no shopping mall!"

The locals must have loved it!

As the disciples all stood there in awe, one of them remembered these words: "Zeal for your house will consume me" (v. 17).

The purpose of incarnation was so we could see the glory of God. As we look at Jesus, we see the love of God, the mercy of God, the joy of God, and the goodness of God. But don't forget, as you watch Jesus, that we also get to see the zeal and the consuming anger of a God who hates injustice and abuse. Our God is a consuming fire, and the kingdom of God doesn't always just blow through the window like a soft spring breeze. Often, it comes only with a vigorous fight! There are times to make a plate of cookies to take to a neighbor, and there are other times to make a scene. People around us need to see what we are for, but it can be just as powerful when they see what we are against.

So what should we care about? What's worth fighting for?

Based on this story, it's clear that Jesus generally didn't have patience for religious bull of any kind. Remember, the most disorienting factor that keeps people from seeing God clearly is religion: empty ritual, overbearing rules, hypocritical judgment of others, rhetoric without reality, worship without good works, and exploitation of people under the guise of faith. In other words, Jesus can't stand it when we try to go vertical while neglecting the horizontal.

VERTICAL WITHOUT HORIZONTAL

The easiest way to tell if your religious experience would make Jesus mad is if you carry on your own private faith between you and God (vertical) without the same focus on the practical, day-to-day love of others around you (horizontal). Brandon Hatmaker, in a book called *Barefoot Church*, reminds us that when we go only north and south, we leave a terrible taste in the world's mouth. Here are a few examples that Brandon brought up.

- The first four commandments are about us and God (vertical), and the last six are about us and other people (horizontal).
- The greatest commandment given by Jesus was to love God with all our heart, mind, soul, and strength (vertical), *and* love our neighbor as much as we love ourselves (horizontal).
- Jesus taught that before you take Communion (vertical), if you have someone who has something against you, go fix the problem first (horizontal).
- Paul taught that husbands should not even pray to God (vertical) if they have mistreated their wives (horizontal).
- First John 4:20–21 says, "Whoever claims to love God yet hates a brother or sister is a liar. For whoever does not love their brother and sister, whom they have seen, cannot love God, whom they have not seen. And he has given us this command: Anyone who loves God must also love their brother and sister."
- Jesus taught that if you don't forgive others, God won't forgive you.

- Jesus went even further in showing that the way we treat others is exactly how we are treating Him. In Matthew 25:45, when talking about giving food and water to the poor, He said, "Truly I tell you, whatever you did not do for one of the least of these, you did not do for me."

- In Mark 10:14, Jesus confronted vertical religion with His buddies: "When Jesus saw what was happening, he was angry with his disciples. He said to them, 'Let the children come to me. Don't stop them! For the Kingdom of God belongs to those who are like these children'" (NLT).

You can see why religion made Jesus so mad and why He was actually moved to action. He knows that church attendance alone, if left unchecked with real involvement with others, turns people into pharisees—and that if unchallenged, this leaven creates a justified apathy that ends up exploiting the people who really need God the most. Religion takes up a lot of time and money and delivers very little. This type of faith is of no use to Jesus, and if Jesus called out His closest friends on this issue, we should consider an occasional integrity check.

I make this critique with quite a bit of caution because I don't want to be an alarmist or a downer on the church that I love. But people outside our faith would stand up and cheer if we would be honest and consider a little good-hearted critique of what we call "church." Let me go further: I'm a huge church lover. I pastor a local body, and I believe that the church throughout history has shown its ability to mobilize people for the good of humanity. Whether involved in social programs, neighborhood benevolence, Protestant work ethic, hospitals, schools, or just good ol' fashioned generosity, Christians account for a staggering percentage of social good throughout the world. Yet as we approach a new world fraught with injustice, hunger, disease, poverty, and social and sexual exploitation—and as the world looks for the true face of God to believe in—I feel we can no longer view the viability of the church through the lens of a Sunday church service. That's simply not the time we do our best work.

Throughout the Old and New Testaments, God was clearly weary of our worship without works of compassion. And just like Jesus with the money changers, we must be willing to fight the natural consumerism of our culture both inside and outside the church that asks us to provide a safe place of spiritual encouragement while millions face daily trauma, sex trafficking, bloated hunger, and treatable diseases.

God designed the church—but not a church that functions for itself. The church is the "people of God," and therefore it shouldn't have to cost that much. Programs, pastors, and sanitized churches cost a lot. Therefore, anytime we let "church" become the recipient of its own giving, we are dangerously close to the same exploitation that Jesus turned over. He wants His church, His people, to be released from all that hinders true love and true help from reaching those who need it the most. I am so proud to know hundreds of church leaders who are courageously reevaluating their level of consumerism and making painful and personal adjustments to avoid the money-changer scenario. In order to gain the respect of the culture around us, I think it's fair to get a little cranky at the cost of organized religion.

Jesus did.

Now that you can picture Jesus picking a fight in a local saloon, it may be easier for you to picture Him calling someone a bad name. Here are a few that Bible translators allowed in—names He called the local pastors of the day who were running the whole religious scam: brood of vipers, snakes, sons of hell (which is quite a bit worse than our SOB), whitewashed graves, and two-faced dead men. Jesus didn't pull any punches with people He knew were going to make it hard for others to find food or true faith.

WHAT TABLE ARE YOU GOING TO TURN OVER?

Apathy occurs when you don't think your time, money, or effort will make a difference. When you stop listening to the cries of the world or looking at the pain in the world, your emotions and passions dull, and you're as good as dead if you let it continue. Incarnation calls you to courageously keep alert and stay available. Most importantly, you really do have to pick a fight or two.

But likely not the kind you're thinking of …

Today I came home and could tell Cheryl really wanted to talk. She poured my cup of coffee and even put it in the microwave. As soon as the microwave beeped, she said, "Meet me in the pub." I didn't even have to ask her how the day was as she just started pouring out her heart. "Okay, so we really need to start praying. I took Bri out for lunch today, and I finally heard the real story of her life. She's twenty-one, and her daughter, Jada, is four. She just got evicted, and her car got smashed in a wreck last week. She takes the bus across town to work at the restaurant, and she has no real help with her daughter. Babe, I know we were about to start another community for our friends, but I just don't want us to spend what little time we have doing another suburban group for middle-income adults when thousands of kids—literally kids—have no family and no one to help them get through life. Let's pray about filling our house with young struggling teens and early twentysomethings." Since that talk we've added two other homeless nineteen-year-olds to our empty-nest home.

The reality is that most of us can't manage more than a houseful of friends. Although we all want to have clean, safe friends to do Bible studies with, at some point someone has to stop and fill his or her house with truly hurting people. I think that was the day God gave us another fight to pick. I think it's time to fight for those who can't fight for themselves.

I don't know what fight you need to pick, but I hope you realize that life will move pretty fast and that someday soon, if you don't find something worthwhile to fight for, you'll be fighting for your spiritual life. God created us to come alive and truly grow deep when we are waist deep in the things He cares about. If you want a safe faith, you will never really know God because He doesn't hang out in the shallow end much. He's a deep God, and deep calls out to the deep.

You really need a fight … for you. And you need to fight along with other friends. We all want community, but the best community happens when we pick a cause or pick some people to help. Christian community happens only in community with people who actively follow Jesus. And if you get some friends to pursue a common struggle, you will find a level of community that you could never find by just looking for friends. Dietrich Bonhoeffer said, "He who loves community, destroys community; he who loves the brethren, builds community." His point is that when people focus on finding Christian friends to huddle together with, they generally destroy the utopia they've built up in their minds, but those who simply love people always create genuine, deep community.

Finally, you need a fight so that people will see God as He truly is. The best witness isn't telling people concepts about God. The best witness of the gospel happens when people see an entire community sticking up for people who are nameless, voiceless, or powerless. Every Jesus follower should be an activist, an abolitionist, or at least an advocate. And every Christian community should find something to make a ruckus about together! As Matthew 5:16 says, "In the same way, let your light shine before others, that they may see your good deeds and glorify your Father in heaven." If you live horizontally, people will look vertically to God.

LEVERAGE THE FIGHT

One person cannot change the whole world, but you can change the world for one person. You also can't change anything quickly—but if you ask God to show you what makes Him mad and breaks His heart, and then take action by making small, consistent commitments of time, money, relationship, and prayer, you will make a tangible difference over the course of your life. Matthew 11:12 says, "From the time John the Baptist began preaching until now, the Kingdom of Heaven has been forcefully advancing" (NLT). Since God knows there's a very real fight between darkness and light, He has called us to fight together. This is the power of "church" actually living like the people of God. They become a "leveraged" community. Leverage is a bunch of people doing small things together to make a huge impact.

I've always wanted to help with the issue of hunger, but for twenty years I did virtually nothing because I didn't trust organizations, didn't think my fifty dollars would do much, and didn't think the problem would ever go away. As I mentioned earlier, when I ran into the folks at Convoy of Hope, I decided to shelve all of my concerns and go expose myself to the needs in Haiti. In just two days' time, I was sold and realized that I could make a difference. I committed to work one day a year for the poor, giving just that one day's wage to Convoy. Then I asked my faith community to do this with me. My $300 combined with another $13,000 and then turned into $130,000 because Convoy of Hope gets corporate matching funds to exponentially grow every dollar times ten. I then recruited one non-Christian businessman I knew, took him to a Convoy golf tournament to introduce him to this NGO, and now Matt is recruiting another sixty real-estate agents to take on the cause and hold another golf tournament. It's called leverage, and it makes every little relationship, cent, and second count in real time. Our ability to change the world isn't just based on us. It's based on our ability to draw others into the same fights we fight. I can only imagine if ten, twenty, two hundred, or twenty thousand of you who read this paragraph work one day for the poor with me, how many millions of dollars and thousands of meals would get to Haiti, Japan, and other areas hit by staggering injustice and disaster.

To check out Convoy of Hope, go to ConvoyofHope.org.

As you consider a fleshy life that matters, ponder who you will fight alongside with and what you will fight for. Find things that make you mad or sad, to the point where your blood boils and tears fall, and get a plan to move forward. Men, call other men to fight the sex-trafficking epidemic by living honorably and committing not to let porn win the day. Millions of young women's lives are destroyed simply because men won't stay off these sites. Advertising dollars are raised by the millions, and more women are destroyed. Call people to Convoy of Hope or other proven relief agencies, but consider making your first investment, if you're able, to go with them and see what they do. I know you'll feel bad spending the money to get there that you could have just sent them, but you will stay with it longer and give more generously if you see real people in their real situations. So plan a trip together and go! Get ahold of Brandon Hatmaker's book *Barefoot Church*, and take a group of friends through an eight-week experience called *Barefoot Church Primer* to find needs in your own community.

You can find these resources at www.missio.us.

The key is to find something you really care about, stick with it, and fight with friends. Your heart will come alive and your credibility will grow—and God will get the glory.

> Live such good lives among the pagans that, though
> they accuse you of doing wrong, they may see your
> good deeds and glorify God on the day he visits us.
> (1 Pet. 2:12)

Think. What could you help abolish? Who can you be an advocate for? What table might you want to turn over?

Feel. What makes you mad? What makes you sad?

Do. What table are you going to turn over this year? Prayerfully decide which cause you can give your life to. Even a few small commitments of your time and money over the years will make a big difference. What are you going to do about it starting this week? Do something.

9

PUBLIC HOUSE

Letting Jesus Dwell in Your Home

People who know me best know that I have a bucket-list dream of someday owning my own pub. As I've traveled, I have enjoyed collecting bar-tap handles and cool decorations, as well as acquiring some historical documents about establishments and their owners. My favorite stories come from old Wild West saloons and Irish pubs. The name of my place will be something like "McHugh's Wildhorse Saloon" or "O'Halterman's Spit & Griddle Public House."

That's what *pub* means: "a public house." What makes a pub different from a bar or restaurant or standard speakeasy is that pubs are on every street or in every neighborhood. Thus, pub culture is about having a place for a localized group of friends or people from a specific neighborhood. And if you've ever traveled and enjoyed a pint in one of these haunts, you quickly see the power of community, friendship, local knowledge, and deep tradition. Pubs are designed to make the public come into the home. Or better yet, to make the home a place for the public.

THE DWELLING

It's time to focus on the dwelling part of John 1:14: "The Word became flesh and made his *dwelling* among us. We have seen his glory." I've read thousands of pages and a truckload of books about the incarnation, and not once have I heard any significant commentary on the fact that Jesus left His king's palace in heaven and moved to the cheapest side of the tracks, bought Himself a little shack next to the rest of us, put a rocking chair on the front porch and a barbecue in the backyard, and became our neighbor. That's big news, and we can't move deeply into incarnated life unless we learn how to do "home" like Jesus did.

Christianity is an Eastern faith, and those in Eastern culture view social space much differently than we Westerners do. In Eastern culture, people let other humans get close. Families are often much larger, people share space much easier, and therefore the concept of hospitality is much fuller than in the West. Although we don't mind putting out a few crackers and cheese, we tend to be more controlled and uncomfortable when people come into our space or overstay their welcome. Our homes, therefore, are much more a place of refuge and privacy than a tool for mission.

So let's see if we can bring a little more Eastern into our Western ways. Consider these encouragements about making your house a pub. (Check out this first guy's name. Go figure!)

There was an estate nearby that belonged to Publius, the chief official of the island. He welcomed us to his home and showed us generous hospitality for three days. (Acts 28:7)

Gaius, whose hospitality I and the whole church here enjoy, sends you his greetings. (Rom. 16:23)

Share with the Lord's people who are in need. Practice hospitality. (Rom. 12:13)

Do not forget to show hospitality to strangers, for by so doing some people have shown hospitality to angels without knowing it. (Heb. 13:2)

We ought therefore to show hospitality to such people so that we may work together for the truth. (3 John v. 8)

You can see that hospitality is not a fringe idea. In fact, as we watch Jesus, we can pick up on a secret that He was trying to teach us: social space creates spiritual space. In other words, when people feel acceptance, they move toward God much more easily. This is why so many of Jesus's stories happened in homes. When He invited Himself into the home of the hated tax collector Levi, everyone freaked out, including Levi, because to enter a home and eat with someone was a neon sign that said, "He's a friend; I accept him." Regardless of the culture in which you live or your personal aptitude, introversion, or extroversion, we all have a God-given ability to create a warm home. It may be tough to get started, but I know that if you start making small commitments to invite at least one person or a couple over a week, you'll soon find that your energy increases because you see how much God will do right in your living room.

WHEN HOME BECAME THE CHURCH

As the New Testament church was born, most people were still leaving their homes and heading to the synagogue for spiritual rituals. For Jewish people, like for many of us, there was a separation between where they did life and where they did God stuff. But Jesus taught that the temple (church building) or temple leaders (priest or pastors) were going to be much less important for the "church" because the church would now be a people and not a place.

After His death, a large number of Jewish men and women became Christians, and as you would expect, they struggled to figure out how their faith in Jesus would sync up with their Jewish temple traditions. So at first they sort of did a little of everything. Acts 2:46 says, "Every day they continued to meet together in the temple courts. They broke bread in their homes and ate together with glad and sincere hearts." The new Jesus movement was alive with vigor, but you could already see the movement from the temple to the home. Eventually, the Gentiles (non-Jews) also began to come to faith in droves, and since they didn't have a tradition of going to a temple or synagogue, a movement of vibrant faith communities sprang up almost entirely in homes.

And people then, just as they do today, needed to learn how to get comfy with this new kingdom value of practicing hospitality (Rom.

12). Paul was one of those Jewish men who did. Paul, of course, after a stint spent persecuting Jewish Christians, had a miraculous conversion. As a cosmic joke to Paul, God sent him as a missionary to incarnate to the Gentiles. Roman emperor Claudius had kicked all the Jewish people out of Jerusalem about fifteen years after Jesus, and Paul, as a relatively new believer, was invited into the home of some local exiled Jews named Priscilla and Aquila. Paul lived with them for eighteen months and learned their trade of tent making while he started a new faith community. Several months earlier, Paul also had a deep experience with a woman in Philippi named Lydia, who invited Paul and his traveling associates back to her place after she became a Jesus follower.

Hospitality isn't just a female skill, but I find it amazing that God was teaching Paul a strategy of reaching new friends by putting him in homes where faithful women could model safety, warmth, acceptance, and conversation. This is why Paul in 1 Thessalonians talks about pastoring this small house church in Thessalonica like a "nursing mother taking care of her own children" (2:7 ESV). The home, therefore, was the place of teaching people how to be a Jesus follower and become a better Jesus follower.

This is why Jesus made His dwelling among us. He had to show us that true hospitality isn't just for us, our friends, or our small groups.

Hospitality actually means "love of strangers."

WHEN YOUR HOME BECOMES HIS PUB

With the excitement of a middle school boy on his first date, I called Cheryl one afternoon to tell her, "Honey, I'm bringing you home a present."

"Take it back—I don't trust you!" she snapped.

"Trust me on this … it's epic!" I begged.

"Now I'm even more worried!" she replied.

Like an exhausted Norseman fighting through the coldest snow-storm to bring food to his family, I carefully navigated my daughter's Ford Explorer through the city streets of Denver to the front door of my casa, transporting a thirteen-foot solid wood-beam Celtic cross from a local pub that had gone out of business. One end of the cross was wedged up against the glass on the front dash, and the last eight feet were hanging out the back window. I had picked it up for a paltry hundred dollars, and it felt as if I had stolen the crown from the king's court.

I was like a kid on Christmas morning.

I slowly pulled into our driveway, gently stopped, and glanced up to see if Cheryl was looking out the window. She was, and she didn't look very happy. Undeterred, I carefully pulled the three-hundred-pound cross from the car and stood it up, and Cheryl was nice enough to snap this photo. Then she left me standing there by myself.

I hauled it into the house, mounted the thing right in the middle of our living room, accented it with lights, and after a few months, Cheryl got used to it. Not only did she get used to it, but she gave me permission to turn the entire barely useful living room into an Irish pub. What a woman!

"Hugh's Pub" has now become a bit of a legend around our community. Guys drop by without asking to sit and watch ball games. I just performed a marriage while standing behind the hundred-year-old Irish bar, and I can honestly say that having a public house has been the single most important incarnational asset we've acquired.

No, I'm not recommending that all of you put a thirteen-foot cross in your house to make it work, but you do need to somehow let Jesus be the center of your house. And if you let Him move in, I guarantee you that He's going to make it a bit more public.

Here are a few pointers for how to get the hospitality mojo groovin' and how to open up your own pub.

OPEN THE DOOR AND PUCKER UP!

We once threw a summer party, and while I was getting some last-minute cuts of meat off the grill, I heard the doorbell ring. I asked one of my guests to get the door. What ensued was painful to watch. Joe moved toward the door but seemed really fidgety. He acted like he was rehearsing what to say. He intently stared at the doorknob, and it appeared that my request of him was beyond his pay grade or life experience. He was a well-paid, highly respected engineer, but this open-the-door-and-greet-the-stranger assignment really had his boxers in a square knot. He did eventually open the door, so I finally exhaled, but then he just stood there. In fact, he barely opened the door wide enough for the poor man on the other side to squeeze through. When the new visitor finally came in, the two men just stared at each other. *Awkward!*

To break the silence I yelled from the back porch, "Joe, just greet Kyle with a holy kiss, and show him where the beers are." My joke didn't make things any better, but it's the best I could come up with on short notice. What did I learn? That apparently it's hard for people to meet and greet strangers.

A few years ago I was traveling throughout the Middle East and noticed that men liked to kiss each other two to three times on the face, some even on the lips. Each time we would meet new people I would do my best, but I was just overthinking the whole mess. *Do I start on the right side of their face or the left? If I pick the wrong side to begin with, it's going to get intimate really fast! Do I actually make lip-to-face contact or just make the facial motions? Do I conjure up the lip-smacking sound or keep it quiet? And what do I do with my hands?* I about had a panic attack wondering how to simply greet people!

Well, maybe it's about time for some kissing lessons. Both 2 Corinthians 13:12 and Romans 16:16 encourage us to make the greeting real: "Greet one another with a holy kiss." I've always figured this was just a cultural thing that we didn't have to pay much attention to, but as I've studied this, I realize the true meaning. The idea of a kiss was most known as a custom between burly, masculine Roman soldiers. As the churches grew and as the gospel brought "strangers" into the communities, to extend a kiss represented mutual respect and acceptance. To kiss other people was to acknowledge equality with them—to show that they now belonged.

I know what you're saying to yourself: "Hugh, I get the point, but I ain't kissing anyone who comes to my door!" I'm not asking you to smack lips, but promise me you'll take the moment of greeting seriously. When people enter your home, the first thing they cross is the threshold, and the threshold is "the place or point of beginning."

A home is someone's most intimate space, and it's just natural to feel like you don't belong. It's always been that way, and so making people feel as if they belong in the first few seconds is a critical incarnational nuance. So if we're not going to give them a smooch, what is the equivalent? Well, I try to watch for them and open the door before they even get there. They should know I was looking for them and care enough not to make them wait uncomfortably. The other thing I always do, if they are new to my house, is to personally walk them all the way in, introduce them to at least a few people quickly, and make sure a conversation is under way before I leave them. This communicates that my new friends are just as important as my old friends. It ain't a holy Roman kiss, but it has the same effect.

WASHING FEET

In John 13, we see Jesus in His last few hours of the three years with His interns. He'd been faithful to do everything the Father had told Him to do, and much of that was to spend thousands of hours with twelve men who might be able to extend His story into the future. He was eating in fear because He knew painful physical death was just around the corner. He was in deep sadness, as He also knew this would be the last time as a man, as a friend, that He would be with these young men. And He was in deep stress as He pondered what was at stake if these twelve missed some of the most important elements of His life. He had good reason to think that they might miss a huge lesson.

Jesus quietly got up while the boys were basking in their high position, went outside to retrieve the small water basin and towel, and returned. All the men must have turned around as Jesus then stooped down at Peter's feet. Some gasped, some started to spit and sputter, and Peter freaked out. And then Jesus washed their feet.

FEET THROUGHOUT HISTORY

The Jewish concept of hospitality came from Genesis 18. Three strangers showed up at Abram's (Abraham's) home, and he washed all of their feet. The three people ended up being the Trinity: the Father, Son, and Holy Spirit. Earlier in Genesis 12, God had called Abraham to leave his homeland and start out on a journey to bring blessing to the whole world. Abraham probably had no clue what blessing people would mean, but he got it right in this account and formed the basis of true hospitality. By opening his home to strangers from this pagan land, he literally was opening his home to God. The concept of welcoming strangers was called *hachnasat orchim*, which meant that welcoming guests was like welcoming God. After this event, washing the feet of strangers who came into one's home became a metaphor for caring for those who had wandered in the wilderness and who could now take off the shoes of daily struggle— literally take a load off. To wash someone's feet was to say, "Let me serve you; you've had a hard day."

When Jesus was circumcised by Simeon in Luke 2:22–35, He would have been lifted high in front of the entire community, and this customary saying would have been proclaimed: "We are not strangers to this child, and we will not be strangers in the future." It was both prophetic and powerful in proclaiming that God was all about accepting people.

In John 12:1–3, Mary, the sister of Lazarus, washed Jesus's feet. To deepen the metaphor she poured perfumed oil on His feet and then stooped low to wipe His dirty feet with her hair. In Luke 7:36–48, Jesus was at Simon's house, and an unnamed woman, who was thought to be a prostitute, also rubbed oil on His feet and added her own tears and then wiped His feet with her hair. Jesus, whose feet were first washed by Abram, the man given the promise of having the entire world blessed through his lineage—Jesus, whose infant feet were washed by Simeon, who was waiting for the Messiah—this Jesus was now being washed again by a family member and a prostitute.

And so, in this final hour of incarnational training, Jesus stooped down and washed His disciples' feet. Peter's response was telling. He was ashamed. It is awkward to be served, especially by someone who is perceived to be above you. But that is the point of hospitality. Like Peter, people don't feel like they deserve extravagant blessing. This is the power of your home. Every time you stoop down to wash the feet of the wandering souls who enter your home, it reflects the central story of God's love for people.

> You call me "Teacher" and "Lord," and rightly so,
> for that is what I am. Now that I, your Lord and

Teacher, have washed your feet, you also should
wash one another's feet. (John 13:13–14)

What does washing feet look like in today's world? It simply
means taking the pressure off people. Have some fun toys or a baby-
sitter for the kids, take your guests' coats, and hand them some food
and drink. Removing pressure and truly honoring them mean personally introducing them to new friends and staying with them until
the conversations become natural. It requires getting past surface
conversation and with total focus asking, "Seriously, though, how
has life really been this last month? Is there anything I can help out
with?" Washing feet isn't just about inviting people into your house.
It's doing everything you can to make your house their house, at least
while they are with you.

HAPPY HOUR

A few years ago, my daughter was dating a young man who was
living with his single mom and her redneck boyfriend Clancey. The
Meet the Fockers moment finally came for us to have them all over,
and I don't think anyone was looking forward to it. My daughter was
pacing like a puma, my wife was a bit on edge, and I was in no mood
to be godly. Clancey was out of work, on the deadbeat side, smoked
like four cords of green wood, and had a nasty temper. The young
man, his mother, and Clancey all pulled up in a classic 1982 Chevy
truck with a different color fender on all sides of the vehicle, and as
I watched the group from the window, I could see that they felt even
less comfortable than we did.

As they came in, I did a bang-up job of greeting them. No, I didn't slap a wet one on Clancey, but I did take his smoldering, smoke-filled jacket and threw it in my office. I then cracked a few jokes to lighten the mood. As we stood on the threshold, the ol' silent awkwardness settled around us. *Quick, Halter, think, man, think!* Nothing came, but my daughter Alli, sensing the tension, blurted out, "Dad, you should show Clancey your pub."

Working like a fine NASCAR team, I leaped on my daughter's brilliant suggestion and said, "Clancey, it's five o'clock somewhere, so if you're a gamer, let's have a little happy hour." Clancey immediately and visibly exhaled (a plume of smoke he had been holding since his last puff on my front porch) and joined me in my pub. I offered pub grub of every kind. Fine crackers and cheeses, nuts, and dark chocolate. I brought in some redneck wiener wraps, and we had a great ol' time. He asked some dumb questions, but we had fun. Looking at the elk head hanging above, he asked, "Did ya shoot dat?" Playing with him a bit, I replied, "Na … one day it just came running through the backyard, smashed into the house, and got stuck!"

I'm not saying we became chums, but I learned that a little happy hour can be a necessary segue to the main course.

THE TABLE

So you have people in now, and they feel comfy. Time to move to the best part of the home—the table. For Jesus, eating with people was the final word on acceptance. It was where the most meaningful conversations happened, and the table became the symbol of true sacrament. That's why we call the Eucharist the Lord's Supper.

On the same night Jesus washed feet, He was reclining at a table, and He took bread and wine and asked the disciples to remember Him every time they sat down to eat. He didn't ask them to fumble a silly prayer before their meal. He asked them to remember this whole night He had spent with them: *Remember how I made a spot for you at the table? Remember how I accepted you, and even some of you who would reject Me and sell Me out? Remember how I stooped down to wash your feet? Now remember Me as you rip bread from a loaf and drink great wine. Everything at the table should remind you of Me.* That night Jesus modeled what He had taught in numerous parables about the table.

It was a picture of heaven.

It was a place of friendship and conversation. It was to be a hope that would sustain them until the end. The table was the place people met God. Clearly, Jesus never meant for this to become a sacrament of an institutional church. He meant it to be more important than that. He would have never wanted it to be used as an instrument of judgment and spiritual control instead of as the simplest way anyone could grab some bread and drink some wine with friends.

So remember that as you open up your house, you are creating a space and an experience that is as close to the heart of God and the life of Jesus as you can get.

If you ever come to eat at the Halters' table, my wife will most likely have created some table setting with your name on it so you know you were thought about before you even sat down. You will never have to worry about keeping conversation going because we will pepper you with questions about your life. Because we want you to feel comfortable, we will have suggested that you invite a friend or two, and we will always share a toast, which will feel strangely like a prayer over your life, without all the religious stuff. Our table also moves slowly. We won't rush through the food and then jam a cookie down your throat. We want you to know that we've reserved the whole night for you. More wine will be poured, and by the time the dessert comes, you'll know you're among friends.

"Whenever you eat, do this in remembrance of Me" doesn't really work if we offer our table only to those we already feel comfortable with. It must be an open table. They called Jesus a "friend of sinners" because He called sinners to the table.

Check out this video we made about setting a table for the world: www.youtube.com/watch?v=PhNqfq_6_68.

YOU'LL NEVER HAVE TO CLEAN THE HOUSE AGAIN

In John 14, Jesus was trying to comfort His disciples about His need to leave them and return to His Father. He said,

> Do not let your hearts be troubled. You believe in God; believe also in me. My Father's house has many rooms; if that were not so, would I have told you that I am going there to prepare a place for you? And if I go and prepare a place for you, I will come back and take you to be with me that you also may be where I am. (vv. 1–3)

In the Middle East, the cities are essentially a connected maze of attached units. The homes are very unlike our normal single-family dwellings; a father or friend would often just build another room right next to the existing home, and so on and so forth. You may not appreciate this level of closeness, but to Jesus's friends, it would have been so warming to know that Jesus was going to actually add rooms onto His place for them. They would be right next to Him, always.

Someday we will never have to open our homes again. God will give us a final home, and we will literally dwell with Him. Right next to Him, always. There will be no more need to clean the house, open the house, or try to reach a friend. We will all be friends and get to chill forever. Let's use that encouragement as fodder to open our homes now.

Think. Are you too reserved, too private, or too concerned about having people in your house? Why? What is the root of the problem? What do you think God might be saying to you in this chapter?

Feel. Describe the best dinner out you ever had. Be as detailed as you can.

Do. Consider starting a "dinner club" with a handful of friends. Once a month, take turns hosting a sit-down dinner where you can learn how to outdo one another both in cuisine and in the overall experience. It will be the best missionary training you do together.

CONVERSATION

Jesus had conversations most of us don't get to experience. Though His words were honest and strong, they were received because people trusted His life. He was a master at knowing a person's story, inner thoughts, and questions, so He used the right words ... or at least something that would unlock more interest.

Jesus came to the world full of grace and truth. Grace came through how He lived, and truth followed naturally in what people saw in His life and in what He said.

Like a mother trying to get a baby to open his mouth to a spoonful of mashed peas, many Christians today view confronting people with "truth" as the highest and most worthy task to be done. We figure truth is good for people, so we just press ahead, without any sense of relationship, context, or timing, all the while missing the way of Jesus. The verse most people use as unconscious permission to accost people with theology and Bible verses is 1 Timothy 3:15: "You will know how people ought to conduct themselves in God's household, which is the church of the living God, the pillar and foundation of the truth." We always stop right there, because if we do, we can justify picketing and pestering anyone we think is not lining up to biblical truth. But the next verse straightens out the misconception: "Beyond all question, the mystery from which true godliness springs is great: He appeared in the flesh, was vindicated by the Spirit, was seen by angels, was preached among the nations, was believed on in the world, was taken up in glory" (v. 16).

The mystery that is being spoken here is the story that Jesus came in the flesh! Among all the other systems of faith, all the contradictory theologies and doctrines that people proclaimed and fought over, Paul was telling Timothy not to quibble or try to forcibly convict or coerce the culture. Instead, the church was to be a community whose main purpose would be to reveal the mystery that Jesus was God and He became a man. The people of God, by both what they say and how they live, are to be a stabilizing presence among all the swirling opinions and bear beautiful witness about the incarnation of Jesus.

In this next section, let's talk about the conversation God would want us to have with the culture around us. It's time to see how grace and truth work together.

10

WHEN GRACE AND TRUTH COLLIDE

How Jesus Got to the Conversation

Before we get to the actual conversation, let's look at some incarnational nuances that allowed Jesus to have the conversations in the first place.

In the fall of 2012, the national news posted a story about a bakery owner who chose not to bake a cake for a wedding between two gay men. Realizing that this scenario held a lot of embedded incarnational questions, I posted this question on my personal blog: "If Jesus was the only baker in town and two gay men asked Him to bake a cake for their wedding ceremony, would He bake the cake?"

In twenty-four hours, I had about four thousand responses. As I took a week to read through them, I realized that the Christian responses were split down the middle. On the side of the bakery owner, most of the arguments were about sticking up for the institution of marriage and not wanting to condone sinful behavior or actual sinners. Many even thought that by withholding the cake, some of the gay community might feel convicted and turn from their wicked ways. So denying the cake would be an evangelistic method to try.

For the pro–cake-bakers, many thought the cake wasn't the real issue and that deciding to withhold business services because we don't agree with someone's lifestyle would lead to a legalistic slippery slope. In other words, if we don't bake the cake, then what else wouldn't we do for people who do not share our spiritual convictions?

Both sides had some well-thought-out arguments and quoted Scripture to support their views. Yet I was surprised that not one person on either side mentioned what I think would have been Jesus's main concern. I think Jesus would simply want to know what He would have to do to get a good conversation going.

We'll eventually propose some options for the myriad of social-spiritual dilemmas that incarnational life will present, but here are a few thoughts about how Jesus handled the gray areas and got to the conversation.

FIFTY SHADES OF GRAY

Christians often think that our faith is a system and therefore always provides a black-and-white answer to every issue. You just have to pick the side you're on. Either we condemn or condone, confront or let people off the hook, befriend or belittle. Some think you should just "love" without truth, and others think you should just "truth" 'em regardless of whether they feel love. What you'll find in the life of Jesus is that He was quite comfortable in fifty shades of gray (not the book), and instead of picking a side, He transcended all the dilemmas, arguments, trite judgments, and religious expectations simply by not picking a side. He neither condoned nor condemned, and yet people felt accepted by Him … and they felt conviction.

Here is an incarnational zinger. Jesus was God and thus the most holy, true, and perfect being. And He was the most nonjudgmental person you would have ever met. People should have been intimidated and afraid to even approach Him, yet they came toward Him. People wanted to hear what He had to say about their broken lives. And when He finally spoke, they listened and changed. Jesus showed that you don't need to condemn a person before that person will change—and that's why He said He did not come into the world to condemn but to save (John 3:17). And He did exactly that. People around Him didn't feel condemned, and they responded to His truth. He was chock-full, buckets overflowing, oozing out both grace and truth at the same time.

He regularly ate with the worst of the worst. Clearly, many would have pulled Him aside and said, "Jesus, by eating with them, You realize that You are causing them to feel a false sense of acceptance by You, right? Don't You think it is wiser to avoid letting them feel Your love, so that they might come to their senses and stop doing what they are doing?"

Jesus responded, "I didn't come for the healthy but the sick" (Mark 2:17, author's paraphrase). Again, He bypassed the "condone or condemn" option by getting to the real issue: in order to help the sick, you have to be with the sick. To talk with the sick, you have to eat with the sick.

In street-level vernacular, Jesus was saying, "Look, I'm the one you are truly sinning against. I'm the one who should ultimately be the most offended by how you live your life. Your sin is what I went to the cross for. It cost Me My life! But I took care of it; I don't judge or condemn you, so let's have a talk." If Jesus, who is without sin, wants to talk with sinners, we who are sinners should be more than willing to converse without condemning.

GOD IS A BIG BOY

Most of the fights I've gotten into, both the school-yard playground spats and the verbal spars with adults, have been in defense of someone else or over a principle I thought mattered. We know that God loves it when we stick up for the powerless, defend the orphan, or fight against injustice. But strangely, He never asks us to stick up for Him. Unlike the people God asks us to fight for, He is not powerless or unable to defend Himself. He is a big boy and isn't concerned about swaying people to His point of view. He has a higher goal: the transformation of the heart. All the other stuff comes later.

To those who say that baking a cake would defile the sanctity of marriage, I'd suggest that we defile marriage all the time. Fifty percent of heterosexual Christian marriages end in divorce, and a good percentage of those who don't divorce defile marriage daily as men cheat on their wives through pornography. None of it is God's intended design. But what is being torn down is not the idea or institution of marriage. The people are the ones being hurt.

Biblical marriage between a man and a woman will always be foundational simply because God designed it to be. And although the "institution" may be corrupted, the essence will always be safe. If someone destroys an unborn child or murders a neighbor or passes new legislation allowing cloning or embryonic research, the lives of people are hurt, but the sanctity of life is still sacred because God has made it so. People of every sexual orientation miss God's design for marriage. In fact, they miss His design for just about everything. It's called sin—missing God's mark. But for some reason, God looks past that and still shows up at our parties, our ceremonies, and our dinner tables.

He wants to talk. He did way back then.

I believe He still wants to talk today.

Jesus shows us that there's never a change of mind unless there's a change of heart, and there will never be a change of heart without a conversation between trusted friends.

SIN'S SLIPPERY SLOPE

After reading more about the real baker, I found myself trusting his motives. He didn't seem to be knowingly judgmental or unloving. In fact, he seemed very thoughtful and caring. I believe he actually felt that by baking the cake he would be causing them to sin.

I've felt that same feeling at times when I'm at a pub and a friend has one too many, or I've invited a few dudes to go fishing only to find out that it caused a big ruckus in their marriages the next day. I don't think any of us want to lead people into sin. As you watch Jesus navigate the gray, He didn't seem to think that being with them would cause them to sin more.

If we lived our lives making decisions about who we will befriend, who we will hang out with, or who we will do business for based on the fear of propelling them deeper into their sin, you can see how crazy that would get. Since gluttony is listed as a sin twice as many times as homosexuality, the baker would be liable for gross negligence for filling the weekly doughnut order for the chunky Bible preacher. As well, the pastor would be liable for the sins of his glutton-heavy congregation every time he brought the platter of pastries into the church. "Yeah, but, Hugh, not everyone in his church is a glutton." Well, you're right, so I guess both the baker and the frumpy pastor would have to arbitrarily look at each person and make the call. "Sorry, Irma. I believe that by allowing you this blueberry fritter, I am contributing to your sin of gluttony."

Since it is a proven fact that a large percentage of the men in our congregations fight addictive tendencies toward pornography, do we condemn anyone who has a computer, helps make computers, or helps fix computers? And do we search high and low to make sure the products we use aren't made or distributed by any Buddhist, Hindu, atheist, Mormon, Muslim, liberal, or fan of *The View*? For if we help them gain even one dollar, we would be perpetuating their misguided ways, right?

"But, Hugh, to be totally honest, aren't there just some sins that are so bad we should call them out? Seriously, being gay must be worse than eating a dozen Krispy Kremes, right?" Here are a couple of questions that may help.

What is worse: Doing something you don't know is wrong, or doing something you know is wrong? You're right if you guessed the latter. Clearly, when people do things that they don't feel any conviction against or don't know are against God's intended design, we would call them blind or lost, but certainly not bad or evil. But what about people who know what is right and wrong, good and bad, and continue to do what they shouldn't or don't do what they should? Well, yes, that would seem to be worse because at least they understand but are intentionally giving God the middle finger. So sins of disobedience are as bad as sins of ignorance. It is a natural tendency to single out certain strains of brokenness and call them worse than what we think our sins are.

That, by the way, is the definition of self-righteousness. That is, we self-assess that our righteousness is better than someone else's or that our failure in right living isn't quite as big a gaffe as that other guy's. Jesus isn't a big fan of this.

Friends, a Spirit-enlightened believer who keeps chowing down on buffalo wings; a man who will not face his pornography addiction; a pastor who fudges on his taxes; a Christian man who lies on occasion to save face; the Christian soccer mom who leaves her weekly Bible study to head to the mall and keeps running up the Visa tab to buy whatever her Oprah magazine tempts her with; or the rest of us who don't take care of orphans or widows or who don't love our enemies or love our neighbors as much as we love ourselves or give up all we have and give to the poor are *no* better or worse than two gay men who in their own brokenness walk in blindness.

Our sins of disobedience are just as bad as their sins of ignorance. There is no sliding scale of brokenness, and if you're going to withhold baking a cake for a gay man, you'd better shut down the whole darn bakery, because no one else is really worthy of your red velvet either!

WOULD JESUS BAKE THE CAKE?

In a very real sense, Jesus did bake the cake. The cake is grace, and He specialized in grace so that someday He could bring some truth into our lives. And He didn't just bake the cake, He shows up to our weddings, too. Consider this scene. Jesus has made the cake and is at the wedding. There of course would be only a very small group of people there. Clergy would have stayed away, associates who may not want people to know they were supportive would have stayed home, family members would have avoided the ceremony because … well, they just don't like gay people. But Jesus is there.

As people start enjoying the cake, someone says, "Wow, this is really good cake. Who made it?" Another one looks over at Jesus, who's helping clean up, and says, "That fella over there. He runs the bakery shop around the corner. Apparently He's a rabbi, too. Sort of weird that He's even here, but I heard that He helped set up all day and has been really cool with everyone."

What do you think happens next? I know personally because it has happened to me many times. I get to have a really cool conversation that begins to move people out of their mess. This story isn't just the story of Jesus or my own experience. Read this email I got from a pastor in Fort Worth:

Hugh,

Thought you might enjoy this story. Last week, we had someone come in to see if they could rent out our event space for a gay reception. The man said, "Someone told me you guys are religious, so I don't think you'll allow this, but we are looking to rent this amazing space for our wedding reception." Our GM told him, "We are followers of Jesus, and yes, we would be happy to rent you our space. BREWED was started to serve the city, so of course you can meet here." The man started crying because he had been turned down by several other spaces in the area. What a great start in showing him that Jesus and His followers are not here to judge him but to show him love. One day, I hope he sees that Jesus is the hope of the world!

Joey

I've taken some time on this because I hope you see again that incarnation precedes proclamation. Grace sets up truth. And grace calls you and allows you to be there and to bless someone as a friend. Like a pro linebacker who keeps his gaze firmly fixed on the quarterback, shucking off offensive linemen flying at him, or like the mother or father who looks past the momentary poor choices and sins of a child so that he or she can sit down and address the real heart issue, Jesus got to have life-changing conversations because He was simply there, right with them.

Here's what we know for sure: If we don't bake the cake, we won't have the conversations, and if we don't have the conversations, we won't have any real hope to see God use us in this person's life. But if we, as trusted friends, can leave a trail of grace and truth, someday that person will come to our porch for a chat.

FROM JUDGE BEHIND A BENCH TO FRIEND OR FATHER ON THE PORCH

To be able to overlook sin, naïveté, ignorance, deep brokenness, or even flat-out, in-your-face contempt for values you hold dear, you have to trade in your judge's gavel and buy yourself a nice old rocking chair to put on your front porch.

In Luke 15, we read the well-known story of the prodigal son.
We easily identify with the son who misused and abused and took
for granted God's blessings, but we rarely identify or see ourselves as
the father who essentially baked a cake, gave it to his son, let his son
go off and make a mess of things, and then waited for the natural
story of sin to run its course. He knew that if he gave his son the
money (cake) and didn't challenge his decisions, the young man was
going to fall headlong into trouble. The father was brokenhearted
and deeply sad, but he knew that if he didn't give the son these gifts
and freedom, he'd leave anyway.

Why didn't the father say, "Son, I know you're going to leave,
sin, and squander all the blessings I am giving you. So I won't stop
you, but I'm also not going to help you either. I will not give you my
inheritance or my blessing"?

He didn't take this route because he knew that someday the son
would need a place to come home to; someday he would remember
how his father had blessed him even though he didn't agree, and
grace would allow a space for redemption. The father didn't like it;
who would? But he knew that at all costs he had to keep the relationship open! He wanted the conversation, and he wanted to be the
person his son came back to when rougher times happened. Grace
leading to truth again!

Jesus doesn't condone or condemn. He has not led people into
sin or helped them sin more. God has not been misrepresented, nor
has He burned any relational bridges. What He has done is become
a friend of sinners, and like the old man waiting on the porch for his
son to return home, Jesus is in the best and only spot to be able to
sit next to a hurting friend or son on the porch and have a nice talk.

People almost always, in times of great personal need, return to those who have dignified their personal journey and given them space to learn for themselves.

Your other option is to be a self-righteous judge, and you will never see them again. Your choice!

For a fuller discussion of the gay cake question, check out my blog post at http://hughhalter.com/blog/2012/08/08/ hugh-bakes-a-cake-would-jesus-bake-a-cake-for-a-gay-wedding.

Think. Why do you think we prioritize truth over grace? How has that looked in your life?

Feel. Consider how you feel when people you don't know confront you on something versus how you respond when a trusted friend confronts you. What does that confirm about grace and truth?

Do. Consider setting a lunch appointment with someone you have written off completely.

11

SPEAKING OF JESUS

Having the Conversation Jesus Would Have

It's sort of strange to mention another book right at the beginning of a chapter, but a dear friend named Carl Medearis wrote a timely book titled *Speaking of Jesus*. One thing I've learned is that there is a way to speak of Jesus ... and there's a way not to.

"Speaking of Jesus." I even like the way that sounds, don't you? I never liked it when someone told me to go witness or give my testimony or share the gospel. All those seemed pretty weird and unnatural, but speaking of Jesus? Now that sounds nice.

Carl has taken me to places you would never think a Jesus conversation would be a good idea. Several years ago, he took me to Lebanon and several other spots in the Middle East. In Beirut we had some chat time with Hezbollah leaders; in Amman, Jordan, we met with Muslim men who had billions of dollars; and in Jerusalem and the West Bank (in Palestine), we met with people who see Western Christianity as a farce and one of the world's greatest evils. But each one of them loved to speak about Jesus!

People will always struggle with Christians and church and things that have happened in the name of Jesus, but amazingly even those who don't know much about His life intuitively find His story and His words something warm to speak about.

We've spent most of the book talking about how to get to the conversation, so let's give a few pages to the actual conversation. How do we speak of Jesus the way Jesus would speak about Himself?

A RUNNING CONVERSATION VERSUS RUNNING FROM THE CONVERSATION

Remember, if you let grace ooze *out* of your life, people will eventually seek the truth *in* your life. In John 11:47–48, one of the religious leaders was feeling threatened by Jesus's growing street cred and said, "If we don't stop Him, the entire city of Jerusalem may follow Him" (author's paraphrase). Because Jesus was helping so many people, He was making headline news and was quickly becoming a man of the people. Yet He never forced His way or His words on the people. He never had to set an appointment or try to go reach someone. They just kept coming to Him.

I don't know about you, but I was always taught to go after people and try to weasel words about Jesus into any and almost all conversations. And although I tried, it just never felt right. Even though my heart was pure, my words always seemed to be forced. For a long season I stopped trying and actually ran from the conversations. But as I now study Jesus's way of speaking, I have found an entirely new way of influencing friends without any pressure.

In 1 Peter 3:15, there is a phrase that many Christians never get to enjoy: "But in your hearts revere Christ as Lord." In other words, don't try to make everyone else revere Him. You do the reverence thing in the quietness of your own life. Then it continues, "Always be prepared to give an answer to everyone who asks you to give the reason for the hope that you have. But do this with gentleness and respect." Jesus and His early followers lived such a public witness of their faith that they expected people to come to them.

People talked about the Jesus followers; as believers lived a countercultural life, they knew people would seek them out. This is why we should be encouraged to speak with gentleness and patience. By the time Jesus conversations are happening, you are a person's friend or respected peer, and you don't ever have to go too fast or try to manipulate the conversation. If you let people come to you, and you speak with such gentleness and patience, you will have a comfortable running conversation that they will always lead.

I personally cannot tell you how freeing this realization has been for me. I've seen so many friends find faith in Jesus, but in the last fifteen years I have rarely initiated the conversations. Although I will ask friends out for coffee to check in on them and see how they are doing, I've learned that there is a true art in letting them lead the conversation.

Now let's talk about what to talk about when they do come to you.

TALK WHEN THE INVITATION IS GIVEN

A young gal named Suzett became friends with a community of incredibly godly young women in our church. They grew to love her and included her in everything, and they committed to deep friendship without any weird strings attached. But they did hope and pray vibrant prayers over her life that someday she would find faith in Jesus. For five years these girls did everything together.

This last year, Suzett's life took a turn for the worse. She got some weird disease that caused her muscles to respond like they were in the early stages of Parkinson's; she had several bad falls; her job had become miserable—the list went on and on. As I heard about each event, I would pray for her and hope that something would capture her imagination and cause her to consider asking God for help. Or at least us.

Then, out of the blue, while Cheryl and I were on vacation in Hawaii, Suzett called us to ask for prayer. "I didn't really know who to call, but I've had some really scary things happening in my home. I have been seeing spirits hovering over my bed, items are flying off of my shelves, and I don't even want to be in my own home anymore." I prayed over the phone with her and then promised to come over as soon as we got home.

Situations like this happen often, and I've become convinced that God wants us to wait until the normal difficulties of life create a natural need to get help. When people get in hot water, like Suzett, they will call, and all you have to do to begin the conversation is talk about what they want to talk about. And then leave it at that. For Suzett it was demons; for others it's a tough spot in their marriage, a broken relationship, or uncontrollable panic attacks. Life has a unique way of punching people in the face, so if you focus on the first part of this book, you'll be in the right spot to receive a call.

TALK ABOUT THE KINGDOM

When we got back to Denver, I went to pray over her home. I called a day before and asked if I might come by an hour early and just talk to her. She was very open and thanked me for being willing to spend time with her. I was so excited to finally have this *conversation*. It felt like the process and events had all led to this day and that even the demons were helping set the stage for a very natural chat time.

I knocked on the door, and Suzett, with a big smile, answered and ushered me into her small living room. I was unpleasantly surprised to meet her two college friends Lucy and Brita. I wanted a private chat! After we introduced ourselves, I asked Suzett if she still wanted me to pray over the home and talk about all the spiritual stuff going on. She said, "Yes." To respect both of her friends, I asked, "Brita, Lucy, are you okay if I talk really candidly about Jesus, demons, and all this other stuff that Suzett has been going through?" Both girls looked at each other, smiled, and then nodded to me.

As we talked, I found out that Suzett and Brita had grown up in the same Catholic school and that both lost their fathers unexpectedly. Lucy had once been a Christian but now was a complete atheist. Something had gone terribly wrong in her story. But they all wanted to talk. As they exposed a little of their stories, I found that their struggles with faith were due to two things: what other lousy Christians had done to them and the pain of what had happened in their lives. Brita, in tears, said, "I just have never been able to believe in a God who would let my dad die so early." Suzett chimed in, "Yeah, I just don't know why God would let me experience all these struggles, physical illness … and now I have demons floating through my house?"

To respond to how they had viewed these circumstances I said, "Thanks so much for giving me a bit more information about what has happened to you. I understand why it has been hard for you to believe in God. I, too, have had things happen that rocked me to the core and made me question everything. But here's something that helped cut through all the confusion.

"Like me, I think you missed the main message of Jesus amid all the religion and struggles of life. Jesus came to change everything in life you don't like. And everywhere He went, He talked about a kingdom of God coming into the kingdom of darkness and winning out. The kingdom of heaven simply means that the way things are in heaven can begin to change the way things are on earth. You probably know that He died on a cross, and that is a key part of the story, but the reason He did that was so that something incredible could happen to people. That's why the main story is called the gospel, which means 'good news.'

"A kingdom is simply a realm where someone gets to reign. And Jesus said life on earth is bad news because it is a dark kingdom ruled by greed, selfishness, pain, poverty, sickness, war, abuse, religious blindness, and death. All this stuff is simply a result of the sin that every person brings into the world, and so when Jesus died for all

our sin, He freed us from having to live according to this old kingdom and makes it available for anyone to live life in the kingdom of
God. In God's kingdom there is none of this stuff. No poverty, pain,
sadness, sexual abuse, self-centered boyfriends, pedophile priests, or
rampant prostitution.

"You are struggling to believe in God because you think all the
bad stuff is from Him, but it's exactly the opposite. You've experienced everything He hates and came to change."

"So why doesn't He just make this all work like that, then?"
Suzett asked.

"Great question," I responded. "The simple answer is that He
loves people enough to give us free will to decide which kingdom
we want to reign in our lives, and sadly, most of us pick our own
kingdoms. So we get what happens naturally. God won't force His
reign on us, but when we give up the reins, His kingdom wins out.
That may be what is going on with all this dark spiritual stuff." I
continued, "But the fight is worth it because His kingdom is so good
for us and those around us."

"So I grew up in a Catholic school, and I never heard any of this
kingdom stuff," said Brita.

"Well, I grew up in church my whole life and even did ten years
of church ministry, and no one told me about this either, so don't
feel bad," I said.

Brita continued, "Yeah, but what you just told me is a big deal,
and if it's true, it would change everything."

"Yep," I replied. "All I can tell you is that if you could wipe your
religious memory clean and just focus on Jesus and His main message, you'd be surprised how things make sense."

This is a true story. Wherever I go I find that Christians talk about everything but what Jesus talked about. We try to talk people into church; we try to defend things that lousy Christians have done; we try to answer all their logical questions; we try to expose their lack of historical knowledge; we focus on morals, political viewpoints, sin, hell, and Tim Tebow—but Jesus just talked about the kingdom of heaven.

Before the next conversation with someone God has intentionally placed in your life, consider rereading the Gospels and the book of Acts and get acquainted with His main message. As you do, you will see how much He talked about it, explained it, and modeled it, and it will help you keep the conversation on something people will always want to talk about. The kingdom of God is *that good*!

TALK ABOUT THE KING

If the kingdom of God is good news, then the King of this kingdom is also good news. Here's some encouraging info that should give you more confidence to have a conversation. Almost everyone loves Jesus! In a complementary book I wrote on the life of Jesus, *Sacrilege*, I made the case that people talked favorably about Jesus because He was sacrilegious about everything. *Sacrilege* just means to remove or peel away religious facades to reveal the real deal. Jesus was constantly doing and saying things that broke down the falsities of religion. He was sacrilegious with Scripture and told the Bible scholars of the day to quit being arrogant about all their knowledge, calling them instead to obey what they knew. He was sacrilegious on the Sabbath, healing people and doing things that made sense to people. He was sacrilegious with social norms and constantly ate with sinners, touched lepers, included little children, and dignified woman. He was sacrilegious with Jewish family customs and taught people that His Father's family was more important than any individual family. And He was sacrilegious with the temple and spiritual leaders, as He destroyed the need for it and them.

He was a true iconoclast, or "image breaker," and although those in power were threatened by Him, the average people loved Him. He set people free and gave them license to live again. He never belittled or condemned people for their behavior, and He was constantly blessing, healing, protecting, and saving people around Him. All this was done way before He did His greatest act of going to the cross for our sins.

Who wouldn't love a man like this? Who wouldn't love it if God was like this?

I was in Washington, DC, last year with a man who has been a chaplain to world leaders. As we talked over dinner, all he did was talk about Jesus. At one point, he got so impassioned, he put down his fork, which had a beautiful piece of prime beef on the end of it, pointed his rickety old finger at me, and said, "Don't waste any more time talking about Christianity, or church, or Christians—just tell people about Jesus!" Then he shared a story about Billy Graham. He said that one day Billy came in to meet him, and he asked Billy, "What, after all these years of incredible ministry, would you have done differently?" Apparently Billy got really emotional and said, "I would have talked about Jesus more." Billy went on to expound about how he had spent his entire life trying to get the whole world to become Christians, and now he realized that was a mistake.

Like so many of us, Billy realized that converting people to Christianity was never on Jesus's agenda, and so it really shouldn't be on ours. He never intended to start another world religion. He never intended to create Christian nations or wipe out other world religions and conquer in the name of Christianity. Jesus simply came to show any person how to be in relationship with the one true God, without any religion!

In John 4, we find a great story of one of Jesus's most profound conversations. He was talking with a Samaritan woman who'd secretly had five husbands and was at a local well to retrieve water. She had three strikes against her. First, she was a woman. Second, she was a Samaritan. Third, she'd had five husbands, and thus she was an outcast even within her own culture. In a small village with nowhere to hide, she was at the well during the heat of the day to avoid everyone else.

All of a sudden Jesus showed up and had a conversation with her. She freaked out and asked Him why He was speaking to her. His response was great: "If you knew the gift of God and who it is that asks you for a drink, you would have asked him and he would have given you living water" (v. 10).

Isn't that amazing? He knew she was a sinner of the first order but started talking about the good news. A gift from God and living water. She knew that, because she was a Samaritan and a sinner, God would never give her a gift. She had been told her entire life that the only thing she would get from God was judgment. But Jesus continued with good news. She bit and became excited to talk about anything spiritual. She wanted to talk about worship, and she loved the idea of having water that would keep her from thirsting ever again. And even after Jesus had exposed that she'd had five husbands, she must have known that His knowledge of her life wasn't thrown out as a condemnation—because as soon as they were done, she ran down the hill and rallied a bunch of people and said, "Come, see a man who told me all that I ever did. Can this be the Christ?" (v. 29 ESV).

Jesus tried to cover His messiahship with most people, but with this woman, who was clearly still waiting for the Savior of the Jewish people, He told her, "I am who you are waiting for" (v. 26, author's paraphrase).

Jesus once said, "I, when I am lifted up from the earth, will draw all people to myself" (John 12:32). Jesus wasn't an arrogant, self-serving God-man. He was trying to help us understand the purity and power of just getting people to Him. As people come to see Jesus as He really is, most of their issues will go away.

So let's remember the four incarnational nuances of speaking of Jesus.

> Keep a running conversation.
> Talk when they ask you to.
> Talk about the kingdom.
> Talk about the King.

As extra credit, I'd suggest you sometimes talk about yourself, but be careful. People expect goofy, sappy personal testimonies that make life sound all rosy. They can smell this flower a mile away, so if you're going to talk about Jesus and yourself, try to keep it real. Talk about what you're learning about the kingdom, what you're learning about the King, and never come across like you've figured it all out and have something you're trying to get them to buy into.

Think. As you consider conversing about Jesus, take a few months and reread all four gospels and the book of Acts, looking for how many times the kingdom of God or kingdom of heaven is spoken of. Make a list of the key aspects of the kingdom so you can become more fluent in talking about it.

Feel. Since the gospel means "good news," consider picking three friends who are struggling, and make a list of what good news might be to them. How do you envision they'd feel if they heard that good news?

Do. Heads up. After finishing this book, I recommend grabbing a few friends—maybe those you've been reading this book with—and set a date to begin using *The Tangible Kingdom Primer* as an eight-week experience in living out the kingdom of God. Go to www.missio.us to find the resource and intro videos. It's your best way to take inspiration and turn it into reality.

CONFRONTATION

As we were driving back down from a day of snowboarding together, Kevin said, "So, my wife and I were talking the other day about how much we love coming over to see you and Cheryl. The thought dawned on us that we hardly ever call you in advance to tell you we're coming. We really should. But we are amazed at how you and Cheryl never seem to fight and your house is always so peaceful."

I laughed. "Always peaceful … are you kidding me? Our house is crazy sometimes. The girls can have some tough moments, and Cheryl and I do have a few tiffs on occasion. We just don't have any of those biggies anymore."

Kevin pressed in, "So you used to fight a lot?"

"Oh yeah, like just about every day. We killed each other the first five years of our marriage," I replied.

"So how do you not fight now? Carol and I are still going at it all the time."

Jokingly, I responded, "Yeah, I know, because every time you come over to our house, you guys are fighting!"

"I know, I feel terrible, but it's like we just don't have a clue how to treat each other, especially in public. Do you have any advice?"

As I stared out the window, peering into the vast opportunities Kevin was presenting to me, I prayed, took a deep breath, and said, "Kevin, I'd love to give you a little advice I've learned over the years, but to do so, I'd have to speak really honestly about my faith in Jesus. Are you okay with that?"

"Yes, of course—that's what I have wanted to figure out; I just didn't know how to ask you."

This conversation is a great segue into our final section of the book. We've taken most of our time to talk about how incarnational life sets up a conversation between trusted friends, but there is one more step we need to get to with people. And that is the divine moment where grace leads to truth and where truth is allowed to confront people with their need for God. We all know that this must happen, but often we don't know *how* it happens. Let's take a look at the mystery of how God brings supernatural "aha moments" to people we've been loving on.

12

THE WILD GOOSE ON THE LOOSE

How Conviction Really Works

Around 8:00 one morning during a weekend trip to see a friend in Vegas, I was enjoying a nice frothy latte at an outdoor café. All the previous evening, Sin City had been in fine form, and I hadn't been able to get any shut-eye because of the constant sounds of drunken debauchery. So I stumbled down in the morning to get a little quiet time.

But that's not what I got.

As I opened a *USA Today* and took a slow sip of java, a man with a megaphone across the street started yelling out Old Testament verses about the judgment of God on the sins of humanity. He must have been a regular to that corner because people just walked by as if he were a fire hydrant. Two gay men holding hands, then a transvestite, then a homeless guy who sat down and started feeding some pigeons.

The "prophet" seemed annoyed that no one was paying attention and then moved diagonally through the intersection and repositioned his shoebox pulpit right next to me. The rant continued. To say I was annoyed would be a gross understatement. There was no one around except him, so I rolled up my newspaper and gently whacked him on the arm to try to get him to stop. "Yo, sparky. I appreciate your fervor, but it's just you and me over here, and I'm a pastor, so I'm good to go on all this judgment stuff. How about chillin' out a bit so I can enjoy my cup of joe?"

He scowled at me and said, "If you're a pastor, you should be doing this with me. This town needs some conviction, son!"

With that said, he flicked the switch back on and continued his Levitical tirade. As I sat there, trying to decide what to do next, my tensions were relieved as a fellow coffee patron walked right up to him and threw a full glass of orange juice right in the man's face and his megaphone! I was so happy! As the preacher bent down to wipe his eyes and clean off the megaphone, I leaned forward and said, "So how's that whole convicting thing working out for ya?"

Although I probably could have been a bit more pastoral in that moment, the question was actually the right one. I'm a firm believer that all people need to be confronted with their sin and their need for God, but how does confrontation and conviction actually work?

To get an answer, we must understand the flight of the wild goose!

In ancient Christian history, there were many symbols for the Holy Spirit. In the Catholic strain of Christianity, from which most

took their cues, it was the traditional dove. A small, docile bird that
flitted about, gently chirping its way through the day. But on a little
island that avoided and resisted the Roman Catholic takeover, a
small but sturdy lot of Irish Christ followers had determined that the
Holy Spirit was much more like a wild goose!

Believe it or not, this is important in confrontation.

In John 16:7–15, Jesus began to teach about the goose.

> But very truly I tell you, it is for your good that
> I am going away. Unless I go away, the Advocate
> will not come to you; but if I go, I will send him
> to you. When he comes, he will prove the world to
> be in the wrong about sin and righteousness and
> judgment: about sin, because people do not believe
> in me; about righteousness, because I am going to
> the Father, where you can see me no longer; and
> about judgment, because the prince of this world
> now stands condemned.
>
> I have much more to say to you, more than
> you can now bear. But when he, the Spirit of truth,
> comes, he will guide you into all the truth. He will
> not speak on his own; he will speak only what he
> hears, and he will tell you what is yet to come. He
> will glorify me because it is from me that he will
> receive what he will make known to you. All that
> belongs to the Father is mine. That is why I said
> the Spirit will receive from me what he will make
> known to you.

Let's digest this a little. Jesus had just told His community that He must leave them. As you would imagine, they were upset, but Jesus told them that it would actually be better for them when He left because He would send the Holy Spirit to them. This Spirit would be an advocate for them, He would tell them what to say and guide them into all truth, and He would do the hard work of convicting and convincing the world of sin and righteousness.

Sounds pretty good, right?

Well, if I was one of the disciples, I don't think that would make me feel better. As friends of Jesus, they saw His incredible power in influencing people. He always said the right things, did the right things, and knew where to go next. The boys had front-row seats to the Master at work but had yet to personally experience any of His power in their own lives. So if Jesus left to go anywhere, I'd probably feel like things were going south. Jesus must have known that they weren't able to comprehend what the Holy Spirit would do in them, so later He told them to stay put in Jerusalem and wait for the Holy Spirit.

As recorded in Acts 2, a small community of believers was waiting in a room. A loud noise—like that of a huge flock of geese—overwhelmed the crowd (v. 2). The Holy Spirit descended on everyone, and they began to speak the words of God in different dialects so that people of every known race could hear the good news in their own language. People were abuzz! Then Peter stood up and began to share the same message in Hebrew to those who understood the native lingo.

> "Therefore let all Israel be assured of this: God has made this Jesus, whom you crucified, both Lord and Messiah."

When the people heard this, they were cut to the heart and said to Peter and the other apostles, "Brothers, what shall we do?"

Peter replied, "Repent and be baptized, every one of you, in the name of Jesus Christ for the forgiveness of your sins. And you will receive the gift of the Holy Spirit. The promise is for you and your children and for all who are far off—for all whom the Lord our God will call."

With many other words he warned them; and he pleaded with them, "Save yourselves from this corrupt generation." Those who accepted his message were baptized, and about three thousand were added to their number that day. (vv. 36–41)

While in John 16 they didn't understand why it was better that Jesus left them, in Acts 2 they, as a community, experienced the power of the wild goose! Here's what they learned.

THE GOOSE IN YOU

I was taught two misconceptions about how the Spirit confronts people. The first was that the Holy Spirit is the one who does *all* the work and we just get to bat cleanup. Sort of like He gets everyone on base, and then we just say a few words over coffee, get a little wood on the ball, and *kabam*, people will fall to their knees in holy repentance.

The other was the opposite. That the Holy Spirit bats cleanup for us. That our job is to speak boldly and babble out anything that might make people feel bad about their sin and fear the flames of Sheol, and that the Holy Spirit's job would be to use whatever gibberish we spewed to help them see what we were talking about.

Apparently, neither is true.

When Jesus, way back in John 16, said it was better for Him to leave in the flesh and send us the Holy Spirit, He wasn't saying that the Holy Spirit would just fly around and do His thing. He was trying to help His followers see that He would now reside in the flesh of His people. The goose doesn't just hover around the world, whispering truth apart from us. The Spirit is actually given to us as a gift and takes residence in us and helps us know what, when, and how to speak of Him. The Holy Spirit is the spirit of Jesus. It's the mystery of the Trinity, and the benefit for you and me is that the goose helps us know how to be more incarnational. His flesh, now abiding in our flesh to help us live a more fleshy life. Here's the bottom line in regard to conviction: people get convicted as they encounter God through us—"Christ in you, the hope of glory" (Col. 1:27).

PROVING THE WORLD WRONG

You'll notice that Jesus said in John 16 that the Spirit will "prove the world to be in the wrong" (v. 8) about sin, righteousness, and judgment. But how does He do this? If the Spirit of God is given to us, then Jesus was saying that He can prove the errors of people's ways simply by how we live truth in front of them. When people see us live less sinfully, they get confronted with their own sin. When they see us live more righteous lives, they see the difference. And when they see us as the least judgmental people in their lives, they will start to understand how God actually judges people. They will be amazed at His grace.

The Holy Spirit, just like Jesus, was not overly freaked out about our sins. But the Spirit and Jesus are both incredibly interested in our sin. What? Sins are things we do that don't measure up to God's design. But sin is the condition of our unbelief. All sins therefore are simply behaviors we do because we don't believe God. When we read in John 16, "about sin, because people do not believe in me" (v. 9), we now understand that God is much more interested in the issue of unbelief than in behavior. So as the Holy Spirit helps us live righteously among others without judgment, people will come face-to-face with the main issue of their beliefs. And when the goose helps them believe, behaviors will change in due time. Remember, even being a believer doesn't mean you believe everything. Our own discipleship means we're learning to believe Jesus in every area of our lives, and since none of us have total belief in every aspect, we can invite others into learning how to believe instead of judging others for their unbelief.

In John 5:22, Jesus said that the Father had given Him the ability to judge people. But earlier, back in John 3, John said that the Father did not send the Son into the world to condemn but to save (v. 17). In other words, Jesus has the right to judge and condemn, but He didn't come to do this. He came to do the opposite. Even with the woman who was caught in adultery, Jesus removed her condemners and then asked her, "Where are your accusers? Didn't even one of them condemn you?" She said, "No, Lord." And Jesus replied, "Neither do I. Go and sin no more" (John 8:10–11 NLT).

Here's a truism we must see in the life of Jesus. The less judgmental we are, the more others will feel a healthy dose of conviction. The more we judge, the less they will feel conviction.

Being convicted or confronted with sin can feel like a sharp finger in the chest, but if we model our lives after Jesus, conviction will feel like a bright light squeezing its way into a dark room. The goal of incarnation is to help people want to be confronted. Here are a few secrets of making that happen.

LET THEM JUDGE THEMSELVES

If you're perceptive when reading the gospel accounts of the life of Jesus, you'll quickly see that Jesus never tried to confront someone. They always tended to confront themselves. Then they would soon come to Jesus to figure out why they felt the way they did.

Our tendency most often is to try to confront people with their sin so they don't get hurt. Not a bad call. It's the logically loving thing to do. But the secret Jesus knows is that most people won't be open to the light until they've tasted the dark.

The woman caught in adultery knew that her lifestyle brought the heat on her. Levi knew that his unfair business practices were causing the locals to hate his guts. The rich young ruler knew that deep down he had no answers for his own spiritual hunger. Jesus didn't have to aggressively confront any of these people. He just had to be there to help them see why it wasn't working out too well.

It's hard to watch our friends and family make poor choices sexually, relationally, or personally. Our tendency is to make them feel bad so that they will listen to godly words of wisdom. But Jesus never did this. He dignified people's journeys enough to let them get into a teachable spot. In other words, a good ol' fashioned mess. The goal of confrontation isn't to make people feel bad. The goal is to help them take ownership of their lives and let God reign.

I know it may be disorienting to see Jesus's lack of confrontation, but God has been doing it this way for a long time. Remember how He clothed Adam in his nakedness after he had screwed up the universe? Do you remember how He restored David after he had slept with another man's wife and killed her husband? Have we forgotten how Jesus sat at the table with Levi, who'd probably stolen a week's wages from the poor the very night Jesus broke bread with him?

Jesus teaches us that helping someone who is in a bind because of his or her own sinfulness is actually the best way to create natural conviction.

Jesus never belittles or says, "You're getting what you deserve." He wasn't the type of guy to say, "I told you so." He was grace and truth embodied, and people flocked to Him to repent and change their lives. Listen to this culminating verse on judgment and repentance:

> God's kindness is intended to lead you to repentance. (Rom. 2:4)

Think. How does this chapter make you rethink how you parent your children or challenge your friends?

Feel. Romans 2 does seem to indicate that we should feel some conviction if we have been judging others. If God is pointing His finger at your chest about judging others, what might that mean?

Do. Let the goose free. Consider who you've been trying to confront. Say a simple prayer over them today, releasing them to the Holy Spirit while asking God to give you ways to be kind.

TRANSFORMATION

As we head toward the home stretch, let's go back to where the story started in John 1:14. We've talked a lot about how Jesus moved into the neighborhood and how important His life is in compelling us to incarnate on behalf of others. We've seen clearly His heart for redemption, but did you know that redemption goes way beyond conversion? The incarnation is really, totally, all about transformation.

Imagine that Jesus moved into your neighborhood and that you became good friends over the years. I'm sure His home would have been the spiritual and social hub or point of reference for the whole neighborhood. As you have come to know Jesus, your relationship has gone way beyond just hanging out or waving to Him as you pass by. I surmise you would have come to realize that Jesus isn't just the coolest guy on the street but the wisest, and on days that you need someone to listen to your deepest longings, bounce questions off, or get timely words of wisdom from, I bet you'd have walked toward His home. You probably wouldn't have to knock on His door because you've learned that He just always seems to be out in the

front yard or sitting on the porch, almost as if He's been waiting to
talk to you, help you, pray for you, and speak to you about things
that really matter. His incarnation therefore isn't just about becoming your friend; He seems to have been sent to help you with your
whole life, the transformation of who you are as a human.

Early on in my faith journey, a friend gave me a little pamphlet
called *My Heart—Christ's Home*. It was just a few short pages, but it
helped me see that at some point we all have to pick up the phone
and invite Jesus over to our house too. When we let Jesus live in our
subdivision, we shouldn't just go to Him for help; we need to invite
Him over and ask Him to renovate every room in the inner life of
who we are. We can no longer just let Him live at a distance as an
encourager; we must let Him enter our home and make it His own.
Thus the incarnation goes way beyond Him making a home next to
ours. The incarnation is about Jesus making His abode in us. This
final phase is what His coming to earth is all about. It's about you
letting Jesus have every room in your house and hoping that as you
incarnate with your friends, they, too, will let Jesus have all of them.
Flesh takes time.

13

FINISHING THE WORK
The Back End of Incarnation

Okay, totally candid here. I'd like to expose the main reason why I still struggle to stay true to the incarnational way of life. Here it is. I know that if I do, people will find Jesus, and then I'm going to have to walk with them ... for a long time!

As we start the journey, a lot of the incarnational nuances are pretty fun, exciting, and inspiring to do. Becoming a cool neighbor, being the party person, having a home that is buzzing with celebration and deep conversations, caring for the poor, becoming less religious, baking cakes for people you normally wouldn't ... they are all compelling aspects of letting Jesus live His life through you. So why don't more people get on with it?

People fight against change, but Jesus came to change everything in us. In the beginning was the Word. All wisdom comes through Jesus; He's the man with the house in the neighborhood, but He's also the one who greets you and sits with you and shares words of life that bring transformation.

The incarnation isn't just about reaching people. That's actually maybe 2 percent of what the whole thing is about. Most of the incarnation is about God breaking into darkness to bring light to humankind, the type of light that brings life, or as Jesus said, life to the fullest (John 10:10). Conversion is a starting point, yes, but transformation is the full heart of the incarnation. It's about people, including those who already have faith, going to the light of Jesus and having their lives continually turned upside down for their own good.

Sometimes we are afraid of what it will cost us later. As we have discussed the nuances of incarnational life, you've probably seen how important patience is to the process. People need our repeated presence in their lives to help them see the glory of God. Yet, even more, the process continues and even lengthens when it comes to someone's transformation. It takes time for someone to put faith in Jesus. It takes even more time for someone's life to conform to the image of Jesus. Therefore, incarnation is just as much about our transformation as it is about our conversion.

Starting the work of incarnation is fun, but finishing the work of incarnation is formidable.

In John 17, Jesus prayed for His disciples, His community. These astounding words came from His deeply emotional heart: "Father, I have finished the work You have given Me to do" (v. 4, author's paraphrase).

We already talked about this a little—obviously Jesus had not helped everyone or even a small percentage of people who wanted His influence in their lives.

Yet Jesus knew His job was finished.

I wonder how you'd feel if you were the last person in line when Jesus said, "I've got to go now … sorry." Probably like the first car that is stopped by the guardrails of a railroad crossing just before a three-hundred-car train. The disciples must have even had a few friends they were hoping Jesus would get to the next day. Surely they had a few more questions to ask Him about the kingdom. But they heard Him say He was done!

So who is going to finish the work?

Yes, you and me!

Jesus had more skin in the game than any of us ever will. He loves people more than we do; He knows the reality and wiles of the Enemy more than we do. He wants to see the world changed more than we ever will. But He had to leave and entrust the workload to us.

As far as business plans to take over the world go, I think we could all agree this one may have been a little too optimistic. The truth is we human-type Jesus followers don't have the bandwidth to handle this. In fact, I find that most people have only enough physical, spiritual, or emotional energy to walk beside a few friends at any one time. So how will God truly reach and transform millions of people?

He does it through community, not individuals.

Incarnation really doesn't work unless it becomes an incarnational community.

INCARNATIONAL COMMUNITY

As I've mentioned, the first book I wrote was called *The Tangible Kingdom: Creating Incarnational Community*. It has been a life's journey to help people see the elephant in the room that most miss.

What's the elephant?

That God designed us to be transformed *primarily* inside a community. There is no such thing as a personal relationship with God. Although you are a person and can relate with God without anyone around, you are not designed to grow by yourself. God inspired every word of the New Testament to point to a community of Christ followers whom He was intending to include in His mission.

Nothing was written to an individual about his or her own life apart from the mission. You can, of course, have "community based" on anything, so when we use the words *incarnational community*, we are referring to a unique band of friends who live intentionally to become more like Jesus together. They share a common story and a common struggle, they confess sin, and they create rhythms that propel them out into the culture as kingdom representatives. They grow deep because they live their deep story together.

You'll notice that Jesus never walked alone. Heck, He was God incarnate, but He moved in the context of incarnational community. As the Father sent Him into the neighborhoods, Jesus took His friends with Him so they would become a community of incarnation.

Take a breather and check out these four ten-minute videos we created to help you cast vision for this with your friends.

To watch the videos, go to www.missio.us/media.htm.

TRANSFORMATION THROUGH TENSION

If you watched the videos, you can see that there is some natural tension in going out on incarnational mission with some friends. It's not just about you anymore. When you follow Jesus, He pulls you away from yourself. Nothing about that process feels good at first. If you're insecure, selfish, can't control alcohol consumption, or have impure motives; if you have blind spots, are insensitive, prejudiced, or hiding some sin; if you don't manage your time well or are always inappropriately late; if you don't tip well, don't listen well, talk too much, are overly spiritual, or are just plain weird around non–Jesus followers, *everything* will be exposed in a community of incarnational saints!

(Thus the main reason why people church hop.)

While you can hide everything in a small group or Sunday church service, in a true incarnational community, you will be seen for who and where you are. This is why Jesus wants us to find some friends to be incarnational with. The tension will force us to be honest, to confess our sins, to carry one another's burdens, and to challenge one another to grow.

THE SPIRIT'S COMMUNITY OF CONFRONTATION

Transformation is about power. Just as we would say that the conversion process is a supernatural experience, we must also realize that transformation is miraculous. The power is the Holy Spirit working in us. Though we enjoy His role as a comforter, we often forget that He also convicts us of sin and righteousness. We usually apply this latter role to Him in regard to helping lost people come to faith, but this same function is the primary means by which He transforms people in Christian community. Through incarnational community, we sometimes hear, "Come on, let's keep going"—sometimes it is a warm word of encouragement, and other times it's a challenge or even a confrontation.

In Mark 10, Jesus was giving His community of apprentices some private devotional time, and they were loving it. Some children, drawn to Jesus, were brought into their "small-group time" but were treated harshly by the disciples. Apparently, the disciples thought that they were entitled to some deeper time with Him. At this point, Scripture says, "He was indignant" (v. 14)! Now that's a strong word. *Indignant* means He was visibly frustrated. Perhaps even spitting mad! Like a coach who has watched a player make the same mistake over and over and then slams the clipboard down, runs over, grabs the face mask, and showers the kid with saliva-filled expletives, Jesus was upset by the actions of His community. And He called them out.

I find it painfully inconsistent that most Christians, while claiming to know how important true incarnational community is, never submit to it. We like the Holy Spirit as our comforter and our guide through our private daily devotions, but we don't let Him call us to align our lives with a band of friends who will speak truth and give their lives with us for the gospel. Sentimentally, we hope that God will change the world and that He will use us, but we move on to the next church at the first sign of conflict, challenge, or hard work.

TRANSFORMATION IS A CONTACT SPORT

In *Forrest Gump*, there's a scene where he is running across the country. In his own words,

> That day, for no particular reason, I decided to go
> for a little run. So I ran to the end of the road.
> And when I got there, I thought maybe I'd run to
> the end of town. And when I got there, I thought
> maybe I'd just run across Greenbow County. And
> I figured, since I run this far, maybe I'd just run
> across the great state of Alabama. And that's what
> I did. I ran clear across Alabama. For no particular
> reason I just kept on going. I ran clear to the ocean.[1]

If you remember the scene, as Forrest ran, people came and ran beside him, and by the time he got to his destination, a huge crowd was with him.

Jesus said that we must learn to walk as He walked, and we have to realize He meant literally walking a lot! Like Forrest, Jesus was constantly moving, and the lessons and experiences that He drew His disciples into happened almost entirely along the way: by the roadside, inside homes He was visiting, or as they ran away from people trying to kill Him. Transformation was not passive or inside safe church buildings. It happened as Jesus taught them how to navigate real life.

This is why incarnational community is so much more effective for your spiritual growth than individual church participation or a great private devotional life. We don't stay put, seated in pews, filling up on head knowledge, hoping that we change by spiritual content osmosis. We move into neighborhoods; we move into one another's lives; and we move into the dark, broken cracks and crevices of human pain so that the head knowledge becomes heart change and eventually gets fleshed out through our hands to the world. Then, just as Jesus did with His community, we sit and process what we have been experiencing together.

Personally, I have found that I will not choose this harder path by myself. I stick with it because I have friends who walk with me as I walk with Jesus.

TRANSFORMATION THROUGH JESUS, NOT JUST GOD

In John 14, Jesus had just shared that He was leaving the disciples. They were freaking out. Their tension level was high because Jesus had just taken them on a three-year journey through some pretty wild country. They knew they'd made it only because they were able to follow a real person. What would they do once He was gone? How would they keep going without an actual face to follow? What would happen if they went back to their generic faith system?

To help them, Jesus said, "You believe in God; believe also in me" (v. 1).

Why would Jesus say this? Well, He knew that a nebulous faith in a distant, impersonal God would not carry them through. It's the same today. When you just believe in God, you retain some spiritual sentiment, but it doesn't call you to anything significant, challenge you beyond where you are, or inspire you to the high call and cost of kingdom living. So when Jesus said, "Believe also in me," He was inviting them to keep the journey personal: "I walked with you as a person; I taught you how to live, speak, and act. So yes, believe in God, but even more, believe and live an intentional life after My life!"

The only way to see substantive spiritual transformation is to view the goal of formation as the development of Christ's life in you.

Remember: "If you claim to be in Him, you must learn to walk as Jesus walked" (1 John 2:6, author's paraphrase). Paul said it this way in Galatians 4:19: "until Christ is formed in you."

This is a call way beyond conversion. It is the call to transformation.

There are no **Think**, **Feel**, **Do** questions here. I believe either you've got it by now, or you don't. I guess the most appropriate thing to do now is to take a walk with God.

SKIN DEEP

The Final Word for Incarnational Natives

You have only one life.

As this book represents my greatest passion and what I think is the greatest need in reviving a movement of Jesus followers around the world, I pray I have in some way given you hope that the result of your life can be much different from what the current trajectory will yield.

To me, the greatest sadness of even an "active" faith life is that it often sets us up to live in solitary Christian refinement. As such, we bear our own image, and most often—well, pretty much all the time—our image fails both us and others. If we can see past this and bear the artistic, altruistic image of Jesus, something remarkably natural and yet miraculous will become the new norm. It may take a little time to get used to, but Jesus's life can have a nice, snug fit in the natural rhythms and cadence of living here on planet earth. Acts 17:28 speaks of this: "In him we live and move and have our being."

Galatians 2:20 makes it more personal: "I have been crucified with Christ and I no longer live, but Christ lives in me. The life I now live in the body, I live by faith in the Son of God, who loved me and gave himself for me."

These words are not the story of a weekend church attender, believer, or religious follower. Instead they call out the life of someone who lives with deep conviction, deep sacrifice, deep faith, and deep influence on the world. God is deep, and as the Psalm declares, "Deep calls to deep" (Ps. 42:7).

In Luke 5, we see Jesus calling His first disciples. A huge multitude gathered around Him, and He saw two empty boats tied offshore. To help the crowd hear Him, He climbed into Peter's boat and then presumptuously asked him to push off from the shore just a bit, probably ten feet or so. I picture an exhausted Peter helping Jesus sit in the boat and then, as the multitude starts to sit down on the shore to listen to His teaching, slowly wading out, holding the edge of the bow of the boat. Jesus would surely have floated away, so Peter must have had to stand there and just hang on while Jesus taught the multitude. We think that was the first time Peter ever really heard Jesus speak. He was a fisherman, after all, and had spent all night working but hadn't caught anything.

I'm not sure if you've ever fished, but if you have, you know that getting skunked isn't a story you want to tell. We always try to lighten the mood by saying stupid things like, "Well, at least we ain't working," or, "A bad day fishing is better than a great day working." But deep down, it's still really frustrating not to catch a fish!

For Peter it was a job, and it must have been weird for him to have Jesus ask for his boat. And even more difficult when Jesus asked him to head back out to deep waters to fish again.

But that's exactly what Jesus does to all of us.

We all say what Peter did: "Yeah, Lord, we've been out all night and caught nothing. They just aren't biting tonight, and our efforts aren't producing much; it's just better to pack it in and mend our nets" (Luke 5:5, author's paraphrase).

For some reason, Peter must have sensed that Jesus wasn't the average guy. And under great fatigue, he obeyed and let Jesus take him deeper. And so Peter pulled his dripping wet self over the worn wooden frame of his vessel, grabbed the oars, and pulled Jesus out into the depths, away from the multitude.

GOING DEEP

Just a quick note. Even though Jesus called Peter deeper, don't forget that Jesus was nice to the multitude. On this occasion, and many others, He fed, taught, and healed the crowds without calling them off the shores. We're not sure why, but Jesus just seemed to love people where they were. Jesus doesn't force anyone to go deep. He will continue to teach, feed, and be kind to the multitude ... and that includes you.

The largest New Testament concept is called grace. And that means you don't have to go on mission for God. You don't have to let Him live your life.

The deeper life, that of letting Jesus live your life, is for those who really want to see the glory of God—for those who want to know what the kingdom is really all about, who understand that the abundant life promised by Jesus is found only when you trade your life for His.

In Luke 5, Peter went deep and threw his nets back out. I imagine that as he started to put the nets out (nets he had just spent hours fixing and untangling), he was probably thinking, *So the water is pretty much the same as it was when we were out here all night. Except now it's the hot part of the day. Instead of putting the nets on the port side, I could just as easily row the boat in a circle and keep the darn nets where they are. The water is still the same water!* That's how most of us think. We see possibilities based only on what we've experienced thus far.

As soon as Peter obeyed the Lord, however, and threw his nets out again, right where Jesus told him to throw them, it was a fish frenzy! Peter had to call the other guys out quickly so they could handle the catch. Peter's friends must have been giggling their heads off as fish flopped all over the place. Although their boats were almost sinking, these men were probably looking at each other, smiling, screeching, and grunting in heavenly levity as they saw the power of Jesus!

But as the other men rejoiced and celebrated, Peter fell to Jesus's feet in despair because he realized that Jesus had given him a second option. Peter came face-to-face with life lived in his own image and power versus life lived in the image and power of Jesus. This was the day he made a first decision to believe in Jesus and also a second decision to live a life after Jesus.

FIRST OR SECOND DECISION?

First-decision Christians are like the multitude. They make a decision to follow Jesus for what He might do for them. They have a belief in God, but they leave it at the level of belief. They may be church attenders, they may love to emotionally sing songs to God, they may love to learn more about God through Bible studies and small groups … but they also tend to prefer to stay on the shore or in the shallows.

Second-decision Christians have made this same first decision, but they head to the deeper water and make a second decision to pattern their lives after the life of Jesus. He was the least judgmental person the world has ever known, so they work to be the same. Jesus loved enemies, served those who would take advantage of Him, had the "outsiders and sinners" as His best friends, and helped remove religious barriers from the spiritually disoriented—so they do the same as second-decision Jesus followers.

First-decision folks take the wide road; second-decision followers choose the narrow road. First-decision humans play it safe, avoid the real world, and wait for God's kingdom to come back. Second-decision apprentices take risks, become natives, and make His kingdom tangible now. First-decision people flow to the currents of what the dominant culture dictates; second-decision leaders intentionally create and hold one another to the counterculture cadences of kingdom life.

BE A LEARNER

As we said in the beginning, becoming a true incarnational native doesn't come easily. Again: "If you claim to be in Him, you must *learn* to walk as Jesus walked" (1 John 2:6, author's paraphrase).

Other than reminding you of key factors of Jesus's incarnation, I have to call you to simply walk with Jesus. You may need to begin by grabbing some friends and putting an initial regimen in place just so you can stretch and grow some new missional muscles. But I think in time, you'll find that the Spirit of God will guide you into all grace and truth. The more you dive in, the more you'll learn how to live. You just literally have to wake up in the morning, invite the Holy Spirit to interrupt your day, and then ask for wisdom in how to follow.

In Mark 10:32, we see the difference between second-decision disciples versus first-decision followers: "They were on their way up to Jerusalem, with Jesus leading the way, and the disciples were astonished, while those who followed were afraid."

Do you see the difference? Jesus always leads us, and there are, again, two types of followers. Are you going to continue to walk behind Him, hearing and reading about Him, going to church gatherings and singing songs to Him, and living in fear? Or will you step up the pace a bit, catch up to Him and His much smaller group of friends who walk to His cadence and see astonishing things?

I pray that you will let Jesus live His life in you and that you will live the life of Jesus. He has taught you how and what to do, when to do it, and with whom you should live this way. It's time for you to hear the words He said to His closest friends:

"As the Father has sent me, I am sending you" (John 20:21).

Go in community, and may that community go in the power of the Holy Spirit.

WEAR JESUS ON YOUR SLEEVE

We started the book with some tattoo imagery, and I'd like to leave you with an image to live with. As I wear an image of the incarnation on my left forearm, I hope that in some way you, too, will wear Jesus on your sleeve. Being incarnational is ultimately and beautifully about displaying God's glory to the world. Jesus came because He wanted the world to know what God was like, and He has given you His life as a reflection of what He knows your life can be about. So don't hide the Jesus you love or live for, but go into the world as He did. And at the end of your earthly story, I hope you will be able to say with peace, "I've finished the work You've given me to do."

Enjoy the rest of your life in the *flesh*.

NOTES

INTRODUCTION
1. Dallas Willard, "Your Place in This World," *The Graduate's Bible (Holman Christian Standard Bible)* (Nashville: Holman Bible Publishers, 2004), 1120.

INCARNATION
1. Jason Mraz, "I Won't Give Up," *Love Is a Four Letter Word* © 2012 Atlantic.

CHAPTER 1: NOSTALGIC GOD
1. Rob Lacey, *The Word on the Street* (Grand Rapids: Zondervan, 2003), 25–26.

2. The Winans, "Redeemed," *Let My People Go* © 1990 Word Entertainment.

CHAPTER 7: WORKERS' COMP
1. Lance Ford, *UnLeader: Reimagining Leadership … and Why We Must* (Kansas City, MO: Beacon Hill, 2012), 69.

CHAPTER 13: FINISHING THE WORK
1. *Forrest Gump*, directed by Robert Zemeckis (Hollywood: Paramount Pictures, 1994).